THE 7th CONTRACT
Making Your Marriage Expectations Come True

A Guide For Discovering What You And Your
Partner Want From Your Marriage And How Best To
Make That Happen

I Linda, with deep
esteem and affection —
Larry   7-14-2021

Larry Losoncy, Ph.D.

The 7th Contract: Making Your Marriage Expectations
Come True

Larry Losoncy Ph.D.

ABOUT THIS BOOK AND WHO
SHOULD READ IT

The 7th Contract: Making Your Marriage Expectations Come True

This book is based on the fact that while married people and people engaged to be married can say what they want and what they expect of themselves and their partner, most of their expectations actually lie just below the surface of consciousness. Most of the expectations only pop up when the situation arises. They might agree that they would like to do breakfast out on Saturdays. But neither give any thought to who should get the bathroom first on a morning when they are both running late.

Marital expectations arise from living, then get stored away as it were, until needed. These expectations are based on each person's convictions about what it means to be a good man, a good husband and lover, a good father, a good woman, and a good wife and lover. That is to say, the man has three expectations of himself and three of his wife. The wife has three expectations of herself and three of her husband. Each of them must come into agreement with their partner and make workable an arrangement that takes account of their six expectations. That agreement could be thought of as the **7th Contract.**

Anyone contemplating marriage will discover in this book the work of love. There are suggestions everywhere about falling in love and how to express and encourage these feelings. This book goes to the next step: doing the work of love. Feelings are the motivation to start the marriage. Doing the work of love is what deepens and sustains the marriage forever. This book puts forth what that needs to be, how to find and keep it going, and the good things that happen as a result. Married couples can use it endlessly. Engaged couples can use it to gauge what they are contemplating for the rest of their lives. Counselors and ministers, physicians, and all who love the couple will find it to be a reliable guide. There is truth to the saying, "Better to have loved and lost than never to have loved." But a better saying would be, "Better to have loved and then loved ever more deeply." The **7th contract** describes how to do the work of love, not just express the sentiments of love.

ABOUT THE AUTHOR

———————✣———————

Lawrence Losoncy Ph.D., LMFT (Licensed Marriage and Family Therapist)

Dr. Larry has been practicing marriage and family therapy from 1976 to the present time. He was a teacher prior to training as a therapist. He continued teaching, consulting, training, and pursuing his own learning along the way. He has published hundreds of columns and articles about family, marriage, and parenting, including 10 years as a columnist for *Marriage Magazine*, a national publication. He also taught marriage and family therapy at the graduate level for Southern Nazarene University in Oklahoma.

Most recently he published three other books available through Amazon Books. **The One Week Manager** speaks to managers of small businesses, family businesses, and work-at-home persons about avoiding or reducing stress in the smaller business setting and in work-at-home settings. Also available on Amazon is his recent book about best parenting practices for parents and caregivers of children in the preschool years, **Those First Six Years.** A third book published earlier this year and available through Amazon books, deals with religious and spiritual wounds: **Wounded: Healing from Religious and Spiritual Wounds.** Each of these books touches on various aspects of life that impact marriage.

Dr Larry is a practicing therapist with Daybreak Family Services in Tulsa, Oklahoma, an innovative and highly regarded agency committed to serving clients on location and with a commitment to family. He and his wife, Mary Jan, have been married for 55 years and have three adult children and six grandchildren.

AUTHOR'S REFLECTIONS

Marriages are miracles of love. Neither magic or simple, no two marriages are alike, and not all are successful. What I have learned from my marriage and from the vast experience of many others is that love and hard work are the ingredients common to all those whose marriages have led to a happiness unlike any other.

What is the single most impressive focus of this wisdom? It is, to me at least, that there really and truly is such a thing as "the work of love." What is this work? How do we do it? That is the sum total of what this book presents. It is work well worth the doing!

I address myself to married couples and to those contemplating marriage, with the hope that many others who support and love the married couple will also read these words. Ministers, therapists, counselors, and "friends of the couple" would be included in this category. Not only must the couple do the works of love: marriages and the people in marriage need all the support they can get. From everyone else in their lives.

The reason for celebrating marriages is that it demonstrates and dramatizes the commitment by all of us to stand by the new couple in all seasons and regardless of circumstances. All of us are called upon to "love, honor, and cherish" the new couple even as they pledge to love each other above all others for the rest of their lives

TABLE OF CONTENTS

ONE
ABOUT THIS BOOK AND ABOUT
"MARRIAGE COUNSELORS"

"Therefore shall a man leave his father and his mother and shall cleave unto his wife: and they shall become one flesh." Genesis 2:24

I TAKE THEE, TO HAVE AND TO HOLD, ABOVE ALL OTHERS, FOR BETTER OR FOR WORSE, IN GOOD TIMES AND BAD, FOR RICHER OR FOR POORER, IN SICKNESS AND IN HEALTH, UNTIL DEATH US DO PART.

This book is focused on what I have found to be useful in working with married and engaged couples. The book is written for couples. It is intended as a lifelong guide, reflecting the best of what has been learned from the experience of others. There is way too much to remember, so the most important points are in bold. Most of what I have written here I have gleaned from other professionals and from couples themselves. I hope that the experience of others, reflected in these pages will prove helpful to you, the readers, in your relationships. I also hope that it will serve a useful purpose to those professionals who scrutinize it, as they "look over our shoulders" in this discussion. We professionals hate to admit it, but we are always curious about "what works" for other therapists.

Marriage counseling and marriage therapy have grown into a discipline during the past fifty years or so, no longer simply a chapter in psychology textbooks. But giving couples advice about how to have a successful marriage is as old as the hills. Observe a wedding reception: people who love the bride and groom watch for their chance to sidle up to one or both of the newlyweds to tell them that one most important piece of advice. Often enough, that advice comes from the experience of the adviser. Even more so, when a married couple have problems, the advice pours in from all sides. If the problem becomes serious, "all sides" become "two sides," and a clan war breaks out. Love for the couple turns into anger or even hatred for one or the other of the couple and the family of the hated one.

Underlying the development of marriage counseling and therapy is a huge amount of information. Then there is an ever-growing amount of statistical analysis, a fancy way of learning from the experience of others by gathering data and then comparing notes as to what it means. There is also a mountain of historical customs and traditions dating back to nearly prehistoric times. There is astonishing new information about how the brain works, what makes us humans tick, what it means to fall in love. Physiology underlies psychology.

Artists, poets, writers, and filmmakers have all given forth about the beauty of love, the greatest and most meaningful of all human endeavors. Spiritual writers and philosophical thinkers have put forth the values, beliefs, and possible meanings of human love, with committed love being described as eternal. I do not suffer from the illusion that I could add anything more meaningful to what centuries of reflections have already given us. The purpose of this book is simply to provide you, the reader, with reliable information about what has worked with other couples. The marriage therapist/counselor is most interested in what works and what has not worked, professionally speaking. Couples and persons looking to become a couple are also presumed to be most interested in what does and does not work for other couples.

Imagine for a moment that you are standing down on the wharf of the old sailing ships, ready to purchase the final maps you intend to follow as you, the captain, set sail. Which maps are the most in demand, fetching the highest price? Only two sets: those of the latest ship to return from the very voyage you are about to begin and those from ships that never returned from the same voyage. You will notice on the maps and charts from the ships that just returned any number of notes and corrections. When you compare these with the maps of those ships lost at sea, you will need to make some decisions. Were ships lost because they followed their maps, or were they lost because they got blown off course? Soon you will think to purchase more maps and charts, looking for those used by other ships that also returned from the journey you are about to begin. What do their notations tell you?

You will also do what you can do to find out about the weather. What would it be like on your anticipated voyage, as compared to what it was like when other captains went on their similar successful voyage? To the extent possible, you will also want to know in what season did those ships that never returned set sail? Unlike contemporary times, those ancient sailors had no radar. There were no professional weather experts. There was no way to detect fronts coming down from the Arctic or up from the Gulf of Mexico. No weather balloons. No networks of meteorologists to construct models of developing storms.

Such has been the case with marriage counseling, officially known as marital therapy. As more and more reliable data has become available, a core theory about how marriage works and how marital therapists can impact that relationship is developing. I say "developing" in the present tense. Even though the core began many decades ago, it will continue developing for many decades to come. What this book has to give you is a status report about what is likely to be of help to you in your marriage or love relationship. It is culled from various sources and the wisdom of millions of couples. Even though there is no "one size fits all" when it comes to how best to do marriage, there are most certainly common issues and identifiable seasons.

For those who are considering marriage, use this book to get a feel for what to expect. Base your decision-making about whether to get married or how to be married, on wisdom gleaned from others who have walked this path. For married persons looking to improve or repair their marriage, use this book to influence how you go about it. For couples who are in relationships but only partially committed, use this book to improve and deepen your love relationship against the day when you and your partner are ready to make a permanent commitment.

TWO
FLEXIBILITY

W hy consider flexibility first? Why not fidelity, love, honesty, or some other important virtue? I start with flexibility because without it, marriages break. "Flex" is the ability to respond to new influences, adapt to change, embrace new situations. To be flexible is to bend but still remain strong like tree limbs: bend but do not break. Flexible athletes and dancers have great strength but also great agility. They can move, bend, turn, and jump but not break. Even concrete and steel structures must be able to give. Otherwise, they will crack, snap, and collapse. Strength alone is not enough. So it is with marriage.

As a marriage therapist and counselor, I am always impressed by the strength of commitment that lovers bring to their marriages. The idea of forever comes easily in love. We commit ourselves forever and, when in love, want our marriage to last forever. But therein lies the trap for many, if not most couples. They love so strongly and commit so permanently that they make the mistake of confusing permanent with unchanging. They pledge their love as though they will never change. Just ask yourself: do you rely on your love for your mate to keep your marriage strong? If you are not married, do you assume that if and when you are married, it will be your love and your partner's love that will keep your marriage strong? If so, you are gambling.

It is not love but the **works of love** that make marriage strong. Better to make a loving commitment to change and redesign your marriage with your partner as needed instead of standing pat on your love. **True: it is love that provides the motivation to get married in the first place. But it is doing the works of love that makes marriages grow deeper and last forever.**

Beyond the notion of adapting your committed relationship to new situations, there is an even deeper challenge that demands flexibility: the loving relationship itself undergoes dramatic change by its very nature! The romantic being in love gives way to a realistic facing up to differences, faults, problems, and conflicts. This part of the love relationship is in turn followed by new security in the relationship—or, if not embraced, the beginning of the end of the marriage. **Human love is dynamic and ever-changing, not static like a statue.**

Flexibility in marriage refers to the very development of your love. Your love is not unchanging. When you fell in love and got married, you were at a beginning point in your love. If you think that your wedding marked the high point in your love, you are making a mistake. You are assuming that your love is set forever. Like a bridge with too little flex, your love will be too rigid. It will crack and break under the weight of life. Two sources of change demand flexibility. They are **adapting to one another** and **adapting to life's events.**

Adapting to One Another: Three Stages

Falling in love requires absolutely no flexibility. It's as easy as falling off the roof. Staying in love, however, is another matter: it demands flexibility. To understand why flexibility is so important to a successful marriage, consider the three states that your love relationship goes through: The romantic stage, the realistic stage, and the secure stage.

The Romantic Stage

During this stage your partner appears far more good than bad, sometimes even all good. Your mate appears beautiful, handsome, attractive, and sexy. Often you cannot stop thinking of the one you love, cannot stop seeing that person in your dreams, hearing that special voice, remembering words the loved one said, how your loved one dresses, walks. To fall in love is to see the other person larger than life: the best person, the most beautiful, the most attractive person you have ever met. This is called **idealizing.**

When we idealize a person, we dwell on their good points, not their bad points. Our perspective about the other person is not balanced. We do not perceive their faults realistically. In fact, many faults go unnoticed; others are considered cute. That is why you may find yourself thinking later on, "My partner didn't do that before we were married." One of the most spoken phrases in marriage is "But I didn't think you were like that." Adding to this natural process is the fact that when we are in love we put our best foot forward, often hiding our faults and sometimes assuming that being in love would make it easy to get rid of our faults for good. Even more serious, for anyone given to blaming others would be the assumption that my partner would be perfect and therefore, "not make me angry."

Also fueling idealization is the tendency to rationalize faults, both our own and our partner's. If our partner is overweight we might decide that chubby is cute or that flabby is tender. We may decide that crude behavior is only being honest. Indeed, love is blind. Another way of not seeing faults is to **discount** them: "I know everybody says he drinks too much. My partner even admits that, but we both know he can cut back or stop whenever he wants to. It's not a problem." "She is a little mouthy now, but I know that once we are married and she is a mother, she will talk in a more respectable fashion."

Once the idealizing ends, we no longer see the

humor, no longer discount the irritations, and pretty much end the rationalizing, sometimes more so about ourselves than our partners. (Note that in Genesis Adam quickly blames Eve.) What to do? The best thing to do is beat on the pillow (not on our mate), punch the wall, make angry speeches that no one else can hear, and then let go of the idealizing. Returning to the real world brings us back to choices. We can give honest feedback to our partner about their failings. We can look in the mirror and claim our own failings. We can change our faults and be supportive of our partner's efforts to change. What does not or cannot be changed we accept, or we do not accept. In recovery from addictions, we pray for the courage to change what we can change, the strength to accept what we cannot change, and the wisdom to know the difference.

When the faults are more than simply faults, such as battering, infidelity, and criminal activity, there is no simple "learn to live with it." There must be significant immediate change or the marriage becomes a nightmare.

It comes as a surprise to people who are in love that they need to be flexible. The whole experience of falling in love is one of unity, a coming together with a conviction that we will be together no matter what happens. The idea of differences and conflicts diminishes when we fall in love. That's one of the reasons why being in love is so exhilarating. But after some time passes, things change. Suddenly it is difficult to live with someone with whom we were head over heels in love with just a short time ago. That's a surprise. A real shocker! The adjustment requires tremendous flexibility. "My wife is not a goddess. My husband is not a god. We have feet of clay!"

I remember a client who, after more than 20 years of marriage, was still angry and disappointed that his wife had not turned out as lovable after their marriage vows as she had been before. Before the marriage, when she disagreed with him, he didn't mind at all. But after they got married, when she disagreed with him he got angry. Further, after their wedding, he minded doing things which she wanted. Even worse, she began to make requests of him with which he didn't even agree. It seemed to him that she was changing. That was unfair. He loved her more the way she had been. How dare she change! He never forgave her. In fact, he was growing to hate her.

The Realistic Stage

The romantic idealizing aspect of love is sooner or later followed by a new time of **realism.** There is a reckoning with one another in more sober terms. Chubby is no longer cute. Anger is no longer to be laughed away. Many couples are shocked at what has happened: there is anger in their relationship! They were so much in love. She was the first person he ever met who never made him angry. He was the first person she ever got to know who understood and agreed with her. It had been assumed by both that to live with and love somebody was to do what that somebody wanted.

Now conflict has broken out. How could they possibly love each other and be angry at the same time? If they are now in disagreement, has their love died? Can we still honestly say "I love you?" Wouldn't that be hypocritical? Most of all, can we still trust each other? Can we trust our love? Have we married wrong? What if I or we had married someone else? What if I have made a mistake?

To love and still not agree or conform with your loved one's wishes is not contradictory. It is a sign that the reality stage of marriage has begun. It is a reminder that there are two individuals in your marriage and in every marriage. **Becoming one in the flesh cannot and does not make one person out of two persons.** It means a physical, emotional union and a new set of unified goals, a shared life. But two persons still! In fact, the marriage relationship supports the individual's personal identity rather than attacking or ending it. The love relationship brings support to each person: support for becoming more and more a person. So the paradox is that there is a oneness in the flesh, a physical union, but that physical and emotional closeness supports the development of more and more individuality as a human being.

Do opposites attract? That debate will go on forever. But one thing is certain: strong unity and love in marriage will make you more and more different! God only made one of each of us. We are unique. Even no two human thumbprints will ever be the same. Love brings our uniqueness to full bloom. Do not be worried about achieving sameness. When the two of you get to be more and more alike as people, something is wrong!

The Secure Stage

We all hear about the romantic stage of love and marriage: the honeymoon, the honeymoon years, the good years, the time when the fire of love burns brightly. By now, you are probably beginning to accept as a fact that the honeymoon time of love ends with realism. A new reckoning sets in, based on reality. But you may not have heard much about the **secure** stage of marriage. This stage lasts for the rest of the marriage.

Secure in the relationship means that as a couple, you are comfortable with each other and the trust between you has become permanent. There are fewer surprises and more familiarity. You have learned what you like and do not like in each other. You understand each other better and have settled most of your disagreements. You recognize that the remaining disagreements probably won't ever get settled, and you leave them alone.

As a couple you have worked through each other's

faults. By this time, you recognize that the faults are here to stay. You do not need to criticize one another because you have come to accept and value each other. You accept the whole package.

The whole package means the whole person with all of his or her strengths and weaknesses, good points and bad points, lovable and unlovable, virtues and vices. Each partner accepts the other, including all that you each might be in the future. From this point on, the two of you will discover, much to your delight, that romance breaks out over and over again! It is as though you are free to fall in love with each other over and over as many times as you wish, yet there is no obligation to do so since you are comfortable with each other and comfortable about your relationship.

The worst that can happen is that you become old familiar friends. You become red hot lovers from time to time, secure in the knowledge that no one is in love every day but that on some days you will be in love while on the rest of the days you will be secure. Another good thing that happens is that you find yourselves free to use your marriage and home as a secure base from which to sally forth, knowing that a safe haven is always there when needed. It no longer becomes a crisis when career demands, business opportunities, or family obligations keep either of you away overnight, a few days, or even for weeks. You know your friend-mate-lover is still there for you forever.

THREE
COMMUNICATION

Neuro-Linguistic Programming (NLP) researchers and practitioners refer to our main channels of communication as Representational Systems (abbreviated to "rep systems"):

- visual
- auditory/verbal
- experiential
- cognitive (superrational)

When we operate **visually,** we take in what happens by making pictures or images, just like a camera. We store them and recall them like photographs. When we communicate, we "give the picture," and "get the picture." We use words and gestures to convey the picture, frequently drawing, outlining, or illustrating with our hands, even if only to make a picture in the air. We will use visual references in our spoken words too: "I'm getting the picture, this is clear, this looks good, look at me when I am speaking to you."

When operating visually, we judge truthfulness and character by the look in the eyes. Words are simply tools to make the picture and to convey the picture. We will drink people in with our eyes and want to see whatever is going on. When not able to see with our eyes, we will take in the sounds, words, and data in order to make a picture in our minds to store in our memory.

When a person operates in the **auditory/verbal** mode, words are to them what images are to people operating in the visual rep system. In this mode, we would judge sincerity by the tone in the voice. We mean what we say. We take others at their word: "That is exactly what you said." "If you don't mean it, don't say it." We expect verbal precision. Choice of words, phrasing, and tone of voice will be the way to convey and perceive character and truth.

When operating in the **experiential** mode, what the person experiences inwardly is the ultimate criterion: "This doesn't feel right" as opposed to the verbal "I don't like the sound of this" as opposed to "This doesn't look right." For the person operating experientially, feelings and vibes matter. The person "senses" danger and puts stock in their "sixth sense." Actions will speak louder than words, but one's sense, instincts, hunches, and gut reactions matter the most.

When operating in the **high cognitive** (superrational) mode, it is the data and the calculating/analyzing that matter the most. The motto here would be to not trust the other senses: appearances can be deceiving, words can be used to fool us, feelings are not a good guide and are not rational. Emotion and experience make clear-thinking nearly impossible. Information, not impressions or hunches, are what matters. If it does not compute, do not trust it or tag it as being the truth.

Most of us have a favored mode of communicating without even realizing it. We will use the mode almost exclusively under pressure and in moments of great enthusiasm, excitement, or satisfaction. We feel most connected with the other person when we both communicate in the same mode, a way of "connecting" in and of itself. When we are operating in different modes, for example, one person analyzing something out loud but the other person wanting to get the picture or hold hands and just feel close, there is little connecting, like ships passing in the night. There is a saying in marital therapy: "Communicating **Is** Relating."

Strategies for Connecting by Communicating

All the time, counselors hear the plea: "Help us to communicate better." Here are some strategies to consider:

Communicate in the same channel as your partner and change to the same channel your partner changes to when your partner changes channels.
Clarify your messages until they are understood. Ask

for clarification of your partner's messages until you understand them.

Give "I" messages. For example, "I feel angry right now" is clear. "A person could become angry listening to what you are saying" is vague and evasive.

Be open to correction, clarification, and improvement. "Some people think this" is vague enough to be true, when the more accurate message would be "This is what I think."

The Christmas carol asks, "Do you hear what I hear? Do you see what I see?" We speak approximately 200 words per minute in ordinary conversational speech. If two people visited for 30 minutes, 6,000 words would be exchanged. In an average day, we probably speak at least 50,000 words and have that many words spoken to us. Our eyes see live instances and video presentations for about 16 hours. That's 16 hours of images, filmed narration, and videos, plus 100,000 words of communication. How much of that communication do we actually receive, remember, and own? How accurately do we process that communication?

How much of the communication between one's self and one's partner actually "sinks in," and how accurately do we process what we receive? Letter and note writing are two examples of how to slow down and carefully process communication with our partner. A great example of doing this is illustrated by a story from a therapist years ago. The therapist wrote about the incident in a marriage magazine: a couple decided that their rural mailbox needed painting. They brought it into the kitchen, set it on the countertop, painted it, and left it there to dry. The wife came into the kitchen the next morning and noticed that the flag was up. Out of force of habit, she opened the mailbox and found a letter from her husband. He had written to remind her that he lived in their house and was married to her, even though she was too busy lately to speak to him. He had asked her out to dinner for the Saturday coming up but not received an answer. So would she please consider this letter an invitation for dinner out this Saturday and RSVP.

Later that day, he noticed that the flag was up again. It was from his wife. Her letter told him how sorry she was and how much she loved him. She also wrote to thank him for caring enough to write since he could not get her attention by speaking. Yes, she would very much like to go to dinner come Saturday evening.

That couple got into the same channel (writing is visual). They owned their messages. They were open to correction. And they improved! That couple reported twenty years and another mailbox later that a mailbox still sits on the kitchen counter. Over the years, everyone in the family has used that mailbox from time to time. With only the two of them at home, the flag still goes up occasionally.

FOUR: UNWRITTEN CONTRACTS:
Hidden Forces in Your Marriage

"Unwritten contracts" are hidden forces in marriage. We could compare them to the contracts between union and management, in which each side comes to the bargaining table with a set of two unwritten contracts. Each side has its own version of what it expects from the other party as well as of themselves. From the beginning, two unwritten contracts exist on each side of the table, from which a single fifth contract is built and signed. When the fifth contract is agreed upon by both parties, it then governs the relationship between the two parties until the agreed upon end date, at which point the process of negotiating a new contract begins all over again.

"Unwritten contracts" is the term Dr. Clifford Sager used to describe the expectations people bring to their marriages. His book on the subject, written more than 50 years ago, is an example of how marriage therapy and marriage counseling began to amass a theoretical base for each new generation of therapists to build upon. It was titled *Marriage Contracts and Couple Therapy: Hidden Forces in Intimate Relationships,* I have used Dr. Sager's concept nonstop for more than 40 years.

The unwritten contracts become apparent mostly when the marriage begins to break into conflict. When people marry, each bring into the marriage their own expectations. These come from their life experiences. For the most part, they are just below the surface of their conscious mind. They cover what each person expects of themselves and of their mate. As these expectations come to light, the couple begin to build out what amounts to a new contract by which they both are guided. This contract never ceases to be negotiated. That is because the unwritten contracts are continuously coming to light for many years, mostly when something happens for the first time in the marriage. "Something" can be anything and everything. What to do when the first child is conceived, how to relate to in-laws, what kind of budget to have: these are examples of literally hundreds of items that come to light as the couple begin to share their lives.

It is these unwritten contracts, these individual expectations that can cause problems in your marriage. The importance of these contracts is that they function constantly in the marriage relationship as standards by which we each guide ourselves and our mates. They often give rise to conflicts, and they are almost always found underneath whatever difficulties and unhappiness you may experience with each other. They lie behind any power struggles between the two of you in your marriage. Do not be surprised by power struggles in your marriage: they occur in nearly all marriages: just part of the territory that goes with sharing life with a partner.

I have been blessed by hundreds of couples who have granted me the privilege of visiting and sharing about how their private contracts came into existence, how they function, and how they affect their marriage. What I have learned from couples is that these hidden forces are indeed powerful in every marriage and **need not remain hidden.** Further, when you and your partner reveal your version of what you wish your marriage to be, **good things can happen**. The reason? Because once the true expectations become known to both partners, it is easy to do something about them.

I have watched and marveled as **power struggles became power-sharings**. Like the phrase implies, "hidden forces" in marriage are strong influences but are mostly unknown until brought out into the light of day. That is what this book is intended to do: to give you the tools for bringing your hidden forces out into the light of day and harnessing them to make a new contract by which you both can be guided.

How They Come About

By the time you got married or will get married, you

have strong ideas about what makes for a good man, husband-lover, and father, and a good woman, wife-lover, and mother. The man will try to be good according to his version. He will judge himself wrong, guilty, or a failure to the extent that he fails his own standards. For example: if he believes that a good husband will protect his woman, he will feel ashamed if she gets insulted in public, but he cannot defend her. The woman who believes that a good wife will keep her husband properly fed will be hurt and confused if her husband tells her that he would rather buy his breakfast on the way to work than eat her breakfast.

These unwritten contracts come from our accumulated lifelong experiences, beginning with our earliest days and continuing to the present time. The way we were treated as a boy or girl, the way we saw other boys and girls treated, the things that we were told, what we observed in men and women: all of these contributed to our slowly emerging identity as a man or woman. Sometimes the influence was in the form of advice or orders based upon our sex:

"Young lady, you will not wear clothes like that." "Young man, you will speak to your mother in a more respectable tone of voice." All of these experiences and messages contributed and continue contributing to the **expectations that you have for yourself and your partner.**

For example: your mother may have prepared 1,000 meals a year for you during a span of 17 years or more. What would the cumulative effect be on you from watching your mother prepare 17,000 meals? If you are a woman, the impact may have been to conclude that a good wife makes breakfast and dinner for her husband, and that a good husband would appreciate same. If you are a man, you may have concluded the same thing, or you may have concluded that a good husband would share the cooking chores with his wife. Nothing dramatic may ever have happened in the kitchen, and neither of you may never have heard even one speech about a "woman's place." But the cumulative effect of those meals left you with some kinds of convictions for yourself and your partner.

What Do Unwritten Contracts Cover?

The unwritten contracts in marriage cover just about everything. Most of "everything" can be grouped into eight main categories:

Money

Sex

Children

Religion and spirituality

Friends

Relatives and in-laws

Use of time

Choice of activities

Take money as an example. No two people think exactly alike about money. Some want to save it. Some want to spend it. You have at least a slightly different idea than your neighbor as to exactly how many dollars you would like to have in your pocket or wallet on any given day. At this very moment, no two persons reading this book likely have the same amount of money on their person. Some like to carry very little, others like to carry a lot.

It is even less likely that any given man and any given woman will think exactly alike about money. Consider that in marriage you and your mate must live together under a common monetary policy that covers **all** aspects of money. This includes how much to earn, how to earn it, how to pay bills, how much to save, what to spend money on, how much to talk about money and with whom, the order of spending priorities, whether to seek financial advice, how to approach tax returns, whether to use credit cards, whether to have a checkbook or separate checkbooks or no checking accounts. The list goes on and on. Be advised: however you decide to handle all things financial, **do talk it out and work it out.** Do not be afraid to discover differences about money matters. Be much more afraid to **not** talk about money matters, no matter how many months or years the conversation may take.

Quiz: Here is a short quiz, connecting this chapter with the next one. This chapter has noted that there are eight categories into which almost all marital expectations fall. Rather than allow hidden forces to control your marriage, this chapter has suggested ways to bring the hidden forces out into the light of day so that each of the married partners can exert more control instead of being driven by past messages about which they are not even aware. The next chapter dwells on the importance of agreeing about who should decide what happens with respect to these eight categories of shared life, yet another avenue for making sure that you **both** run your marriage.

Score: On a scale from 1 to 100%

What percentage of power do you each have? **Money**
You _____ your spouse _____
What do you think the power % should be?   You _____
your spouse _____

Sex

Where is the power?   You _____ your spouse _____
Where should it be?   You _____ your spouse _____

Children

Where is it?   You ____your spouse _____
Where should it be?   You ____your spouse _____

Religion and Spirituality

Where is it?   You _____ your spouse _____
Where should it be?   You _____ your spouse _____

Friends

Where is it?   You _____ your spouse _____
Where should it be?   You _____ your spouse _____

Relatives/In-Laws

Where is it?   You _____ your spouse _____

Where should it be? You _____ your spouse _____

Use of Time
Where is it?   You _____ your spouse _____
Where should it be? You _____ your spouse _____

Choice of Activities
Where is it?   You _____your spouse _____
Where should it be? You _____ your spouse _____

Is The Power Where You Want It?

"Power" means different things to different people. We live in a very powerful country with a very powerful history. Our culture includes violent entertainment. The daily news reports murder, rape, and violation of personal rights almost as frequently as the weather forecast. Beyond living in a culture of violence, we also are surrounded by trauma-inducing events ranging from personal tragedies to natural events such as floods, violent storms, earthquakes, fires. Because of technological genius, these are portrayed graphically for us nonstop. No small wonder that each of us react to "power" with a very wide, long, and deep range of memories and emotions ranging from negative to positive.

"Power" in this discussion of marriage as a relationship simply refers to how much influence each partner has in the decisions that affect them both. "Power" in a love relationship is a bottom-line issue. In marriage, it is absolutely essential that the power issues be addressed freely and openly and, most importantly,

frequently. Remember, the idea of being life partners is that both of you are always on the same side when it comes to your life goals. Like bath towels, "life goals" in marriage include "his," "hers," and "ours." Both persons **always** work to support all three sets of goals.

The goals included as "ours" demand power-sharing based on mutual agreement. This is the territory covered by the eight categories of marital expectations that emerge in the final contract, what I am calling the **7th Contract**, because it is the 7th contract for each partner in each of the eight categories of shared life. Unlike the previous unwritten six versions, it is the one we consciously agree to and remember.

The image of this would be the overlapping of two large circles. If each partner were symbolized by a large circle, their sharing of their lives would be represented by the overlap. There are only so many ways that two people can share their lives, as described in the eight categories we have been discussing. The image is simple. It could serve as an easy way to locate your conversations and decision-making about the items that make up your shared life.

Within the enclosed eight categories, the center of the overlapped circles is the part of your life that you share once married or in a committed relationship.

FIVE
MORE DETAILS ABOUT THE UNWRITTEN CONTRACTS

Money

Both persons bring to the relationship a host of details that mostly only become conscious as the occasion merits. Some of the big-ticket items are the "cost of living." Rent, car payments, food, clothing, vehicle maintenance and repairs, gas, utilities, taxes, savings come to mind. Eventually, there may be mortgage payments, costs of furnishing or buying a home, health insurance, and a variety of other insurance bills such as long-term care, life insurance, and car insurance.

Beyond the obvious, a host of smaller items also pop up from time to time, especially the first time. Each will discover they do have an opinion about how much to spend on things such as Christmas gifts for each other and for others such as parents, grandparents, siblings, and friends. They do have ideas about when and where to vacation, how much to spend on vacation, on eating out, on entertainment. They may have strong convictions about how much credit is proper, who should balance the checkbook, and whether to shop online. Even the "right" amount to tip a waiter, or waitress, or parking attendant may show up in their unwritten contracts.

If they are lucky, they may have money to invest. Investment, retirement, and savings all need to be discussed—many times.

Sex

This category, like the other seven, should be considered broadly. It is not only about when, where and how, and how often to have sex. It's also all about being affectionate, how to talk about sex, whether sexually-oriented jokes are acceptable, how sexy to dress, who initiates.

Children

This category includes whether and when to have children, how many children, how to raise children, discipline philosophy, whether children should have allowances, and zillions of details that start to be considered if and when there are children. Even such items as what time is bedtime are there but often not discovered until the situation arises. You may frequently discover that you do not totally agree on discipline. Should you set a time for children to go to bed? What should you do when they want to stay up past their bedtime? One of you might take the view that children will go to bed when they get sleepy, that every rule has exceptions and some TV programs are worth staying up late to watch. Flexibility would be the watchword.

The other one may take the approach that a rule is a rule: routine and good order make for stability. Parents are supposed to resist the instincts and impulses of children by supplying the willpower they lack.

You may also have as part of your unwritten contract the assumption that a good man in our times is the leader and disciplinarian of the family; that a good woman supports her man even when she disagrees with him. Or you may have the conviction that each of you is a person and should express disagreement when you do disagree. You may think that parents should always present a united front or that your children should be allowed and encouraged to take an active role in developing the rules and sanctions that make up their discipline package.

You may or may not believe in physical punishment or in any punishment. You will almost certainly discover surprises in your thinking when your children become teenagers. Should they be allowed to use your car? Should they have a curfew? Would they ever be grounded? What kind of grades should be acceptable once they are in secondary school?

There was a fifteen-year-old girl who was pregnant by her boyfriend. One parent wanted the youngsters to marry, while the other parent wanted the couple to break up. Who was right? Should they have encouraged the young lady to keep her baby and help her raise it, or should they have opted for her to adopt the baby out? Should they have spoken with the youngsters about their situation more in moral terms or in psychological terms?

Separate Friends

Detailed material about issues in the various other categories of our unwritten contracts also comes to light when situations arise that evoke a needed response. For example, regarding spiritual or religious matters: what church to attend? Whether to attend church at all. How much involvement?

Meeting and making like-minded friends is one of the major reasons that people attend church. Making friends triggers more discovery of unwritten contract material. Many therapists advocate three sets of friends in marriage: her friends, his friends, and their friends. Separate sets of friends are support for each of you in the marriage, providing a source of support and a place to turn when either spouse needs a time-out from each other. However, not everyone will agree with this.

You may have decided from childhood that when you got married, there would be no outside friends and only couple fun. Your motto might be: "We will play together or not play at all." Perhaps you noticed one of your parents hurting the other parent by maintaining unacceptable personal friendships. On the other hand, you may be determined that there should be more emphasis on individual friends and activities from observing your parents suffocate and restrain one another. You may feel that a real man goes out with the boys or that today's woman gets out with other women and does not depend on her husband for fun times.

The issue of who should have what friends, as well as what you should do with friends, comes up early in marriage. That makes sense. After all, most of us had friends long before we met or married our spouse. Our spouses also had friends. Getting married does not equate with dropping friends. Ideally, friends become part of the support system that every couple need. That's the reason they are invited to help celebrate the wedding. But the unwritten contracts about friends can be filled with many more surprises.

Should he golf with the boys? Should you join the ladies' bridge club? Should you bowl with people from the office or only as a couple? Should you take separate vacations with friends? Should one of you go with friends on a weekend outing while the other one must stay home to work or to watch the children?

Should you as a couple or as individuals be friends with your children, putting activities with them over activities with your adult friends? Should fathers be more friends with their sons than with their daughters? Should mothers be closer to their daughters? When your children grow up should you become their adult friends? Most marriage counselors consider becoming adult friends with our adult children to be a key transition in our relationship with them, a way of emphasizing that we have finished parenting and for our adult children, a letting go of their dependency on us.

But the question is, do you agree with the theory? If you agree, how does that play out? Should fathers go camping, scouting, or fishing with their sons? Should mothers go along? Should mothers go shopping with their daughters? Should fathers go along?

I know of a couple who have developed a new contract (**7th contract"**) about activities they share with their daughter. On Wednesdays, the father goes out to dinner with his daughter while the mother takes the night off. On Thursdays, the mother takes the daughter out to dinner while the fathe has the night off. On Fridays, mother and father go out to eat together with their daughter. This **7th contract** takes account of the father's conviction that he should be friends with his daughter and validate her. It also reflects the mother's conviction that she should provide special opportunities for her daughter to meet with her, woman to woman.

Relatives and In-Laws

You are likely to discover many detailed variations in your unwritten contracts about relating to your relatives, in-laws, and their friends. Sometimes things can get complicated.

"Honey, my mother has invited us for Thanksgiving dinner."

"Do we have to go?"

This conversation and many variations of it get repeated for years about Thanksgiving, Christmas, Easter, Memorial Day, the Fourth of July, Labor Day, Sunday afternoons, Sunday evenings, Saturday nights, family get-togethers, picnics, reunions, visitors from out of town, and birthday parties. Just when you think you have everything settled once and for all, a new twist will develop, new considerations will emerge, new conflicts of loyalty will arise, or the situation will change. Should a father and son cancel their day of fishing because grandmother expects the whole family for dinner? Should mother go to her in-laws for a holiday when she would rather be with her own parents? Should you as a couple have the right to your own Christmas or Thanksgiving when the rest of the clan has always gathered for a family Christmas or Thanksgiving? Is it acceptable for you to take an out-of-town ski trip and skip family holidays altogether?

Choice of Activities and the Use of Time

Unwritten contracts have much to say about choice of activities and use of time. In my growing-up family, men always cut the grass. We were a family whose roots went back to the peasant farms of Europe. I do not believe that a woman had ever done the haying in our family during all of those centuries. I never saw or heard of any woman in our clan's large number of women, including grandmothers, aunts, and girl cousins, **ever** mowing even one lawn! It just seemed natural for me as a boy and then as a man, to mow the lawn. Nowhere in the Bible or in any laws does it say that only boys and men should mow lawns. But I assure you, that duty appears in my unwritten contract! And so today, I worry about grass, snow, leaves, weeds, shrubs, and peeling paint for the same reason.

My sense of being a good man, a good husband, a good father tells me to take care of these things. When I let them go, I feel irresponsible, guilty, uneasy.

One way of discovering such hidden forces is by violating these unwritten "ought to do" messages. Many times, couples will discover their conflict to be at this point: one of them, in obeying an unwritten contract duty, is causing the partner to disobey one of their unwritten contract duties. For example: if my wife's unwritten contract told her to mow the lawn, but my unwritten contract told me to mow the lawn and not allow women to do that kind of work, my wife would object. She would feel guilty if I took over the lawn mowing. I would feel guilty if she took over the lawn mowing.

Every aspect of everything is covered by the unwritten contracts we carry around in our subconscious minds about marriage. Anything you could possibly think of in the categories of money is covered. So, work constantly to find, reveal, and consider your unwritten contracts as well as your mate's. You will discover a total of 96 such contracts: (what it means to be a good woman, wife, mother, man, husband, father) in eight categories. From these 96 unwritten and partially hidden sets of expectations, you and your partner will work to achieve **one** set of agreements for each of the eight categories. The sum total of these eight agreements will constitute your "contract" that guides your marriage: **the 7th contract.**

The Process Never Ends

We never lose all those unwritten items in the unwritten contract. In fact, we go on discovering new items as long as we live. Beyond discovery, our unwritten contracts change as we continue to experience life and to learn. That is to say, the **7th contract** is an agreement, made in bits and pieces over time, that continues to evolve. Unlike business contracts, it is not written down, signed, or witnessed. It just becomes the way we do things—until a disagreement leads us to reconsider and make changes.

When you and your partner develop your **7th contract,** do so from the perspective of getting as much out of your marriage as possible. "Win-win" is the way to go. As an example: if you have children, they need to be raised in a way that reflects the best thinking of both you and your partner. In this same vein, what you do with your time, what you do for fun, what you do with your friends and extended families, and where you go on vacation need to be reflective of both of you.

What is unchanging about marriage is that it is a lifelong commitment with no reservations and all the exits closed. Therein lies the secret and the key to success: "permanent but negotiable."

SIX
RULES AND POWER

———————— ❧ ————————

"**R**ules" in marriage refer to the ways you and your mate get things done. After you have been together for a time, you will notice that there are right ways and wrong ways to do almost everything. There may be a right time for dinner, a right way to make the coffee, a proper time for being late getting home before you need to call, even certain words with which you greet each other.

For some couples there is an implied rule as to which side of the bed you sleep on, including when you sleep away from home. These are referred to as rules but, in fact, are simply established procedures: how, what, when, and in what fashion you do things. When they are violated, there is trouble (time to check your unwritten contracts). There may also be rules about rules: established procedures by which rules get made, certain conditions under which rules can be suspended or violated without penalty. Some rules get elevated to the status of all-important and never to be violated, while other rules may have the status of minor.

Rules are a good indicator of where the power lies in any marriage and family. Whoever makes the rules has power. If you both make rules, power is shared. If only one of you makes rules, power is lopsided. Make sure you share power by both of you participating in the rulemaking.

The Good and the Bad of Rules

Rules do not necessarily need to be a problem in marriage. They are, after all, quite useful. They guide us to the proper way of doing almost everything. They will become a problem, however, when either of you dig in about them or when you let the rules become too rigid, too much of a burden, too controlling. They also become a problem when only one of you makes them. When this happens, a power struggle usually results. Power struggles are always deadly, hurtful, damaging, scary. So: rules gone about properly are good for a marriage, while rulemaking that gets out of hand becomes a menace to the marriage.

Rules start as soon as two people begin dating. Look back to the days when you started dating. You will probably recall that even on the first date, each of you began to set rules about how certain things would get done. These may have included who was to call whom, when and how long to talk on the phone, who was to ask for the next date. Other rules may have included how far it would be proper to go on a date, who was to buy, and who was to drive.

As our relationships expand, so do the rules. By the time we are married, most of us know quite well what would and would not irritate our partner. Many more things get discovered and become "rules." Who does the cooking? Who does the dishes? Who makes the bed? Who does laundry, grocery shopping, pay the bills? Who takes care of the car or cars, cleans the house? Who balances the checkbook?

Problems with Rules

When there are rules, problems are big. Sooner or later rules do get broken, changed, or ignored. That instantly tests the power behind the rules. These are important moments in the life of a marriage. The long-range implications about trust and confidence that each of the partners are fair gets put to the test. Further, these moments decide whether or not rules will be flexible and changeable. The question to be decided will be, "Were we made for the rules or were rules made for us?"

Jane came to the appointment in tears, telling me that her husband was a psychotic monster because he had become overbearing and controlling right after they got married. He showed a complete change of character: a total surprise. He could not be reasoned with. He just became more and more angry, screaming that he was not going to let any "b....." run him around by the nose. As it turned out, what her husband had actually done was to tell her that if she didn't like the way he cooked when it was his turn to cook, she didn't need to eat it.

When Jane let it be known that he had hurt her feelings, he didn't offer to kiss and make up. That was the really serious breach since they had always kissed and made up when there was an argument. But this time, he was so angry that he would have no part of making up. Nor did he wish to discuss the matter the next day. Within a week, their problem had deepened to the point that he was staying out late without telling her or explaining why, thus, violating another already established rule in their new household.

Jane's husband was already experiencing a Catch-22 about rules. If he obeyed the rules, he would be hiding his anger, and he would be hypocritical. That would be violating yet another rule, the super rule, that they would always be honest with each other. They would never just humor or patronize each other when an important point was at stake. On the other hand, if he refused to keep the rules, he would be saying in effect that he didn't care about Jane.

There is no avoiding rules in a love relationship. However, because they are so closely tied to trust and love, breaking rules can quickly propel the marriage into a crisis. For this reason, the rulemaking needs to be both honest and continuous, allowing for "brutal honesty" and plenty of negotiating as each partner discovers more and more of their unwritten contracts. One of the interesting realities of marriage is that many couples whose marriages have lasted for many years and who are happy with their marriage, like each other only slightly more than half of the time. How can this be?

The answer is that their relationship has become so trusting that it no longer depends on being "likable" all of the time. On those days when secure persons do not like their partner, they do not need to hide it. The partner who is not liked is also secure enough to allow their partner the right to feel whatever they feel. The world goes on. There are other people to be with and other things to do until such time as the liking of each other returns. Therein lies the true value of "rules." Sticking to the rules is the work of love and the strengthening of trust, not the "likability" factor. In one-on-one relationships, it is impossible to be likable all of the time. But being honest about the rules and being open to listening and changing rules is always possible. That is how trust is built and nourished.

To read or hear about rules all sounds so simple: work together on the rules, be fair, and everything will be fine. But rules are not always simple. Even in the best of marriages, there are so many rules, some discussed and negotiated, but many simply arising from habit and becoming "the way we do things."

How to Work with Rules

Keeping an eye on your rules and rule problems is a normal part of marriage maintenance. It is something to be done regularly, not just once. You would not feed your lawn or fix your yard only once, expecting that to do the job for the next 40, 50, or 60 years. Taking care of rules is like that: not a one-shot application but an ongoing process that needs regular attention. We change, the world around us changes, our "unwritten contracts" change: so the **7th contract** also needs to change. What follows are suggestions based on the ways other couples have successfully gone about taking care of power and trust in their marriages by taking care of their rulemaking:

Watch for Trouble

There is trouble brewing when either of you start to feel like you are in a Catch-22 situation. This happens when you face a decision where both keeping a rule and breaking the rule will bring on trouble. Another sign of trouble is when one of you starts making the rules enforcing the rules, or punishing infractions of rules. We all have a little bit of judge, jury, hangman, supreme court justice, district attorney, and warden in us. Once in a while, these pop up, a sure sign of trouble. It means something is wrong about the way you or your partner are doing things. Something seems unfair, unjust, or someone is taking power, and someone is losing power.

Check out what rules are involved and where the power lies. Check out how each of you are feeling and what you are thinking about the issue. It should only take a few minutes to do this. Do not drift into an argument, keep it short. Listen more than you talk. When this simple rules-check doesn't help, it may mean you are **locked-in about power.**

I remember couples over the years who have made this point graphically. They asked what I, as their counselor, thought was fair. Each time a rule or rule change was proposed one or the other would ask me was it fair? If I said yes, the other partner would become angry and hurt, saying that I had sided against him or her. If I said no, the one who proposed the rule or rule change would accuse me of siding against him or her. This is called "triangling," one of the psychological games couples play when things go wrong. In triangling, the person feels a loss of power (control, security, love, well-being) because it seems like they are alone but that their partner is getting support from one or more other persons. These other persons may be your children, friends, relatives, or a professional such as a doctor, minister, dentist, attorney, or therapist.

When a power struggle is going on, the feelings of being ganged up on, threatened, and wanting someone to agree with us will be very strong. That leads to triangling: a sure sign that the problem is no longer about rules but about **power.** It is about power when we keep trying to get supportive people on our side and involved in the conflict as our ally instead of discussing and negotiating a good solution to the problem.

When you find yourselves involved in a power struggle, do a power roundup. Find out where is the power, who has it, how much of it do they have. This can be on a point-by-point basis or on an overall basis. Use the power distribution chart to do a quick power check, paying close attention to each partner's perceptions as to where they perceive the power to be and where they would like it to be. If you cannot achieve consensus regarding what the percentage of power needs to be on any given point, **set it temporarily at 50/50 for the time being, then come back to it at a later date.** Do not simply continue the discussion because that will instantly become an argument. No good comes of running gunfights, figuratively speaking. So do not start one. Arguments are the last step before an out and-out warfare dynamic. The warfare dynamic is hostility: the only way to win is to defeat the enemy. In marriage, partners are always on the same side, supporting each other's goals and working together at shared goals. There is no room for attacking, much less winning or losing to each other in this relationship. You are **never** each other's enemy, remember?

Power in marriage simply means the ability to make

things happen or not happen, to **determine why, where, how, and when things get done or not done. It does not mean control. Individually and as couples, we all need all the power we can get. We also want the power to be rising, not falling.** Rules, both official and implied, spoken or not, help that process to happen.

Guidelines and the Importance of Rules, Rulemaking, and Power

1. Are the rules fair?
2. Can the rules be questioned?
3. Do each of you know how the rules can be questioned?
4. Can the rules be changed?
5. Do each of you know how the rules can be changed?

Are the rules "published?" If the only way to discover that a rule exists is by breaking it, the rule is not published! Translation: do not make up rules on the spot, and then hold your partner to it. A typical example: after you talk on the phone, your partner says something like, "You should tell me who was on the phone. I shouldn't have to ask you." Since you did not know that such a rule was in place, if you tell your spouse the answer, you are accepting the rule. Now it is published! If you do not tell who it was, it is still not a rule. Unpublished rules pop up all the time. "You should have called." "You know I do not want you to go out with that friend." "You know we never go on vacations with anyone else." "You are home too late."

Rules make life together very easy. They guide our behavior. They smooth things out. With rules, we know what is expected, what is fair, what should happen, what we are comfortable with, where the limits are, and where we stand. They are both a convenience and a guide: grease between the wheels.

Power is a resource which assures us that we can get things to happen or not happen: that we are neither helpless nor prisoners, that we are in control of our destiny. When rules and power are comfortable, we can relax, feel secure, be confident, have less conflicts. Rules tell us what to do when one of us wants the thermostat turned up, but the other one wants it left alone or turned down.

Rules and the use of power raise the question of meaning. "What are we trying to accomplish with our marriage? What is it for?" If the answer is no more than "Conceiving and raising children," the question would be, "But then what?"

SEVEN
CONFLICTS IN MARRIAGE: HOW
TO "FIGHT" CONSTRUCTIVELY

Conflict and love: do they go together? Absolutely! Do most couples realize that conflict is an opportunity to help their love grow? No, they do not. Our culture is strange when it comes to love and conflict. We tend towards so much violence that we assume conflict leads to violence. Because love is so precious, we then also assume that one sure sign of love ought to be a lack of conflict. I cannot count the number of couples who have expressed guilt and shame for being in conflict with each other. We seem to get surprised, shocked, and guilty when we find ourselves squared off against the one we love. Saying in the same breath, "I love you, but I do not agree with what you want" seems hypocritical. "I won't do what you want" seems even more shameful.

How many times, on the other hand, have you assumed that your partner should do what you want as a sign of their love? How many times have you assumed that you should do what your partner wants if you really mean it when you say you love your partner? It is in these two respects—what we expect of our partner and what we expect of ourselves towards our partner— that we tend to measure love and guilt about the love relationship. For many people, the solution lies in the idea that we should sacrifice what we want in favor of what our partner wants. Sacrifice will often enough be necessary—no argument about that. It truly is a sign of love to make sacrifices on behalf of those we love, of course. We would sacrifice a fun day out with friends if our partner were home sick and needed us there. We would sacrifice our savings to pay the cost of getting medically necessary help for our loved one.

But and this is a very important "but," it does our relationship no good to routinely ignore our own needs in favor of our partner's needs, especially if those needs are more "want" than need! Nobody gets married to **not do** the things they want to do, enjoy doing, or would like to do. Further, nobody should get married with the expectation that their partner's every wish is to be accepted as a command. At that rate, neither partner would ever utter the phrase "What do you want? This is what I want." The expectation in such an arrangement would be that we get married so that the other person will take care of us. Parents must take care of their dependent children. But when we get married, it is assumed we will take care of our self. We are not getting a new mother or father when we get married! Those who marry on the false and totally unrealistic expectation of "being taken care of" are doomed to misery.

Much better and realistic would be the recognition that when married, we are still two distinct, unique persons, each with our own life. The marriage is a way of sharing the life that each partner is living, the "overlap" described in the eight categories. That overlap can be as large or as small as the couple make it. When they attempt to make it a total overlap, they will smother each other. When they commit themselves to always support each other's goals for the life that each of them live, it's a partnership. The test of love will never be always doing what the other person wants. Rather, it will be a partnership when each person's needs and wants are always considered and always supported. Therein is where conflict is most likely to occur from time to time. There will always be limits as to how and how much support any partner can give the other partner without giving away themselves. "Conflict," in this context, is "loving conflict." Loving conflict is far different, totally different, than a warfare dynamic. In warfare, the object is to win by destroying the opponent.

In loving conflict, the object is to be as helpful and supportive to each other as possible. Both persons count. Both persons need to be able to look back and honestly declare that because of our marriage, I am better, and my life is more fulfilled than if we had not gotten married and committed to each other until death did us part.

Consider this scenario. A couple is enjoying coffee and the newspaper on a Saturday morning. She asks him what he is planning to today and he replies, "Go fishing or play golf."

"I guess you'll be taking the car?" she asks.

"I plan to," he answers.

"I was planning to go shopping today and have lunch with my mother."

"Can't you go some other day?"

"Can't you play golf or go fishing some other day?" she replies.

"That's not fair."

"Neither are you fair," she replies. "My shopping is just as important as your fishing and golf. Take the car, I'll just stay home!"

And so goes the disagreement, ending in anger and hostility as she stalks into another part of the house. When two people fall into conflict, it is the beginning of a warfare dynamic or an opportunity. There are only so many possible outcomes. In the scenario just described, she turned the opportunity for jointly creating a new rule into a negative game, first taking the victim role and then the persecutor and then back to the victim role. The discussion should never have been about fairness. It should have been about a solution that would have brought both persons to a solution for solving the transportation problem.

The most desirable outcome would be to search for a "win-win" solution, ending the warfare dynamic by nipping it in the bud. This couple could have ended it by his calling a friend to pick him up or her calling her mother to arrange a ride. Or one could have dropped the other one off.

All but "win-win" are negative solutions. The other remaining possible endings are all negative. One half of the couple could "win" the argument, making the other one lose. Or, vice versa, the other one could win. Or they could both lose, deciding that in the interests of being "fair," neither one would do what they were planning to do with the day. They might call this a compromise: making sure that neither one would do what they wanted. Compromise is often portrayed as a way to be fair. Far from being fair, it is a truly negative solution. How can making sure that neither one of us gets what we want be called fair? It is the ugliest thing possible!

Competitive sports are not the model for loving conflict. Competitive sports are an imitation of war: the object is to win. The best way and only way to win a war is to defeat the enemy, i.e., the opponent, in the pretend war called a game. Sporting events are agreed upon warfare, done for fun and entertainment. Loving conflict is never agreed upon warfare done for fun. Vince Lombardi, the famous football coach, once said that "Winning is not the most important thing—it is the only thing." Couples do not get married to "win" but to thrive together in mutual support. **"Loving conflict" is loving and productive.** Both of you win.

Loving our partner is intended to make us both even more of an individual while also strengthening our relationship. We become better persons when we are good towards each other. No two of us are alike. It is said that no two human thumbprints are exactly alike. Imagine: billions of people and not even two tiny thumbprints alike! How much more do we find our uniqueness in our spirit, our mind, our attitudes, perspectives, and our total identities. To grow is to become even more who we are meant to be. The longer we live and grow, the more different we become, in the sense that God made only one of each of us. Why should this not be the case in marriage as well?

"Two shall become one" certainly does not mean that from two loving people, there **emerges one person! It means a shared life, but there are still two persons.** Bear in mind: so long as two individuals live together, they will have differences. You and your partner will be in conflict for as long as you are mates. You have no choice about conflict: it **will** occur. Our only choices are about what kind of conflict we will have. What will it be? Win-Lose, Lose-Win, Lose-Lose, or Win-Win?

What Makes for Good Fights?

Yes, there is such a thing as good fights. Good fights are realistic, fair, specific, aboveboard, two-way, and humorous. Here, in summary form, are the key ingredients of a good fight:

1. **Realistic vs. imaginary**: It is imaginary to fight about whether one of you would remarry upon the death of the other since the fighting is about something that has not happened. It **is** realistic to fight about who told Mother that she was unwelcome in our home.

2. **Fair vs. unfair:** It is unfair to try to hurt the other person physically or emotionally. The purpose should be to resolve the issue. The purpose should never be to hurt the other person physically or emotionally. It is also unfair to figuratively hit below the belt, to declare one's belt line to be above the waist up around the forehead. What is fair is to ask for an explanation without making accusations.

3. **Specific vs. general:** "You should be more

tolerant" is general. "Please give me 10 more minutes to finish cleaning the kitchen before we leave" is specific.

4. **Aboveboard vs. hidden:** Refusing to have sex because you are angry but denying your anger is hidden.

5. **Two-way vs. one-way fighting:** One-way fighting is blaming, persecuting, badgering, manipulating, nagging, playing martyr, or being a victim. Two-way fighting means **both** of you get into it and stay in it. By stalking into another room, the person is removing themselves from the fight. This maneuver keeps the partner from responding and making the fight two-way.

6. **Humorous vs. grim:** Constructive, healthy fighting is often interrupted by laughter because humor is always just around the corner. Do you laugh as together in the middle of your conflicts?

Healthy Fighting

Your fighting is healthy and good when good things result. Here are some good things that happen when couples do their conflicts in a healthy manner:

Hurt is decreased.

Information is gained.

Ground is gained.

Fear is decreased.

Trust is increased.

There is forgiveness and help when hurt.

Self-worth goes up.

Affection and closeness increase.

The air is cleared, and both of you feel relieved.

Couples sometimes fight not to get something solved but to hurt their partner. Have you ever done this? Have you ever been the victim of such fighting? Regarding hurt, the whole point of loving conflict is that such conflict is for the purpose of solving and resolving problems, not as an opening to hurt your partner.

I sometimes hear husbands say that they have never beat up or battered their wives. They take pride in reporting that they have slapped their spouse only once or twice when things got out of control. Wives tell me they only hold back on having sex for a few days when their husbands get out of line. This is hurting!

When hurt starts to build up, you will find yourself keeping score or "gunny sacking." That is, collecting and piling up the hurts, wrongs, and injustices you feel are being inflicted upon you. When the score is sufficiently lopsided against you, you then feel justified in striking back. The war will be on, and the win-lose, lose-win approach will have been set in motion. Perhaps you will do this over money or affection or withholding of other amenities, not just with sex.

He: "She has denied me sex for the last time. I feel

justified in having an affair. That will teach her a lesson."

She: "He has put me down in front of other people at the last six parties. Tonight, I will fix him good and proper by telling everyone what he has been doing with his secretary." It is good conflict when there is healing, not more hurt: when important new information is gained.

He: "Oh, I didn't realize how worried you were about our finances. You will be glad to hear about our new profit-sharing plan." It a good fight when ground is gained. She: "Now that we have put all this out in the open, I feel a lot better about our marriage. I realize how we are gaining ground on our problems. Thank you." It is a good fight when fear is decreased, and trust is increased.

She: "You are such a wonderful, clever, intelligent man! I really respect you and feel safe with you, even when you seem strange about things."

He: "You are such a caring, competent woman! I am proud to be your husband. I'm never afraid that you are about to leave me or hurt me."

It is a good fight when conflict is faced and resolved. And, as a result, forgiveness, self-worth, and affection go up.

She: "Do you remember when you told my father

to get his nose out of our marriage and keep it out? I was so embarrassed and angry. I felt caught in the middle. My father and I had always been so close. He was the one person I could always count on until I met you. Then I had two people I could always count on, two great men. I assumed that you and Dad would become good friends. It surprising to discover that you did not like him. It was even more surprising to find out that you didn't agree with very much of anything he said. When you told him to leave us alone, I thought I had to make a choice between you and him. That is why I got so angry that night and screamed and yelled.

Now I am grateful that you held your ground and didn't back out of that fight. It was because you were willing to stick to your guns and have it out with me that I was finally able to see that it was Dad who needed to accept us both and let us run our own marriage. I still do not like the idea of conflict, but now I realize the value of it. And I trust you even more because I realize that you are willing to say what you think even when I might get angry at you for saying it."

It is a good fight when, as a result, the air gets cleared.

She "You have been moping around here, pouting, and acting like a martyr for two weeks. Each time I ask you what is wrong, you say nothing. If you have something to say, spit it out."

He: "Yes, I do have something bothering me. You won't like it but here goes anyway. You are acting like I am a war criminal because I stayed out late two weeks ago and wouldn't tell you where I was. I resent that I need your permission to sneeze. I'm not a child, and I don't need to give you an account of every move I make. I don't ask where you have been when you come home from an evening out. And you don't tell me. I don't like the double standard."

She: "Well!"

He: "I feel better now that I have finally said it. This double standard has been eating at insides ever since we got married."

Return now to that Saturday morning scenario. Instead of stalking out, she looks her husband in the eyes and says: "I get steamed every time Saturday rolls around. I never know what you are planning. We agreed to have only one car so that we could save the extra money. But I feel absolutely humiliated to beg for the car as though you were my father."

He: "Well, sweetheart, I have to admit I assumed you could work out your ride arrangements."

She: "That's right. You assumed."

He: "I am sorry. What do you propose?"

A Few Rules for Fighting

1. **Be sure the topic is clear.** Many a couple have gone up in flames over something about which they were in agreement, to begin with. Comments such as "That is what I meant" and "That is what I said in the first place" mean that the fight started before the topic was clear.

2. **Stick to the topic.** Stay away from ". . . that reminds me of another thing." It is a mistake every time because it takes the focus away from the first topic, making it much more difficult to remember what was said and agreed upon. Further, it opens the door to gunny sacking: a running gun battle: the participants figuratively keep shooting, in the hope that sooner or later they will hit the target.

3. **Impose a time limit**, no more than 15 minutes. At 300 words per minute, that is more than enough time to say and hear enough. Remember, it is a conversation, not a flogging.

4. **Do not call in other witnesses or authorities.** It is your fight. Keep everyone else out of it. Translation: no comments such as "Many experts say . . ."

5. **Make sure the verdict is clear**. "You are right, I am sorry."

6. **Kiss and make up.** Shake hands, go for a walk, do something to indicate and assure yourselves that there are no hard feelings.

Score Your Fights

Use a simple 0 to 10 rating scale to describe your fight once it is finished. A score of 10 is great, a score of 0 is terrible. Scores that are somewhere between 0 and 10 show you where there could be some improvement. On a scale from 0 to 10, was the fight:

Realistic as opposed to imaginary? _____

Fair as opposed to unfair? _____

Specific as opposed to general? _____

Aboveboard or hidden? _____

Two-way or one-way? _____

Humorous or grim? _____

Now also score your fight for the effects. While it may take a little practice and some self-discipline, the goal would be a score of 10 on each and every item, with the exception of accidentally saying something that was not intended to be hurtful but that turned out to be hurtful. Any time that happens, stop the conversation immediately and take care of the hurt.

On a scale of 0 to 10 did your fight result in:

1. **Less hurt or more hurt?**
2. **More information or less information and more confusion?**
3. **Ground gained or ground lost?**

4. **Less fear or more fear?**
5. **More trust or less trust?**
6. **Forgiveness or resentment?**
7. **More self-worth or less self-worth?**
8. **Air is cleared versus more tension?**
9. **More affection or more hostility?**
10. **More love or less love?**

To Sum Up

Conflict can be a creative and constructive part of our love relationships, essential to an enduring marriage. When a marriage is not constructive, it almost always becomes destructive. There is not much middle ground between constructive and destructive in human relationships. Since it is impossible for two people to live together without conflict, it is advisable to get those conflicts out into the open and then get them settled. Even though I am not standing in front of you at your wedding reception, here is my advice boiled down into a short list:

Conflict and love go together. Do the conflict well, and your love will grow.

It is not hypocritical to love someone but still not do what they want.

Fighting can be good for your love relationship if it is done in love.

The win-win approach to conflict is better than

sacrifice or submission.

Humor is a sign of good fighting.

It is never justifiable to intentionally hurt your spouse emotionally or in any other way.

Forgiveness, increased self-worth, and affection go together when we do our conflicts well.

EIGHT
THIRD-DEGREE BURNS: GAMES THAT HURT

Games People Play is the name of a very famous book, written by Eric Berne. Unfortunately, most of us have played some of those games much too often. Marriage presents constant temptations and opportunities to play psychological games. The one-on-one relationship is very demanding because there is no wiggle room. We have only three choices about a committed love relationship when things go sour. We can grit and bear it, we can work to fix and improve it, or we can bail out.

The one-on-one relationship provides daily choices. Be open or be hidden, generous or selfish, build up or tear down, trust or be suspicious, be vulnerable or defensive. Couples often play games when they have disagreements that are not getting into the open. A psychological game is in progress whenever the conversation stops being honest, when nothing is getting accomplished, or when either one of the couple begins to wonder where they stand with the other. Anger and hurt are building up.

All games boil down to the one basic game of **victim/persecutor/rescuer.** This is the mother of all games, some variations of which are described in this chapter. The deadliest games in marriage are **affair** and **divorce.** When conflicts get out of hand in the marriage, the basic game takes over. When games go on long enough, they all tend to turn deadly to the relationship, ending the affairs or the marriage or both. Everyone involved walks away with wounds.

Everyday Games That People Play

Games are like crabgrass: they multiply and spread. If we play one, we probably are playing other games as well. Here are some common games—perhaps you could think of others:

Now I've Got You: In this game, you lure your partner into the trap of guilt and then pounce, feeling righteous that you have a legitimate reason to be blaming.

"I thought I asked you to get milk on your way home this evening." (victim)

"You did ask me."

"Well, did you?"

"No, I forgot."

"Why do I ever bother to ask you?" (persecutor)

Sending the children to ask your partner why we cannot take a vacation this year when you already know that your partner is too sick or too overworked to take the time off is a form of **Now I've Got**

You. Tricking your partner into revealing in front of relatives or friends a strongly held position with which you disagree and with which you know they will also disagree, is another form of this game.

Flirt: this game has numerous variations, all of which get attention at somebody's expense. Flirting is a way of shaming your partner.

Fix Me, I'm hurt: in this game, you seize on a real or imagined hurt as a weapon by which to get your spouse to do something for you, usually something your spouse does not want to or has refused to do. Sometimes a spouse will manipulate their partner into fighting and hurting just because they like to kiss and make up. If you use fighting and getting hurt as a way to get sex and tenderness, you are   playing this game. It is better to skip the game and simply ask your spouse for sex and tenderness. An even healthier way to get tenderness is to give tenderness.

Ain't It Awful: in this game, the person complains in order to get sympathy or reassurance that things aren't so bad. It would be healthier to let your spouse know that you are feeling afraid and would like some assurance and protection.

Brag: "I'm so wonderful! Look what I have done! Aren't I something!"

Browbeat: in this game, you nag until you get your way.

Doormat: in this game, you let your partner walk all over you. (And then often enough demand that he or she pay a price for the privilege.)

Kick me: a variation of **doormat.** You encourage your partner to hurt you in order to appear more righteous than your partner.

Ignore: also known as "**cold shoulder**," this is a form of punishment.

I'm Hurt but I Won't Tell You Why: another form of punishment. "I will hurt until you cry."

Pout: "I will suffer until you realize that I am hurting, you insensitive monster."

Sob: "I'll bleed emotionally until you rescue me."

Devastated: "look what you have done to me."

Helpless and Hopeless: a demand for rescue.

Look What I Put Up With: a demand for rescue.

What Do You Want Now?: designed to make the other person feel petty.

I Don't Need You: a bluff.

What Would The Neighbors Think: no way to argue with this one. A game of vague demand.

Prude: no way to argue with this one or even be sure what it means.

Know It All: a subtle insult, implying that your partner is stupid but does not know it.

Smug: another implied statement that your mate is stupid.

Above It All: an attempt to stay out of the conflict, not risking anything but being poised to blame.

All-Knowing And All-Wise: a variation of Above It All.

The Basic Game: Victim-Persecutor-Rescuer Affairs very often produce the basic game of victim-persecutor-rescuer.

Example: One morning, the husband called to tell his wife to ignore any mail that might come to her from a certain person. That day a letter arrived, addressed to **him.** It was marked "personal." The wife went to pieces, suspecting the worst. That evening she confronted her husband with her suspicion: "Are you having an affair?" He admitted that he was having an affair. But he blamed her (persecutor), telling her that the reason he did it was because she was such a lousy sex partner, a prude, reluctant to ever enjoy sex. (persecutor) He went into a defensive tirade (victim) concluding with "You make me feel like a rapist." (victim)

She asked him why she had never heard this before. She apologized for her "unwifely" behavior and admitted her shame (victim). He then told her he could teach her how to be a real lover (rescuer).

"Sure you will" she replied angrily, (changing from victim to persecutor). "You are having an affair, and now you are going to make a lover out of me! You are despicable!"

Then it was his turn. He got in a final shot by turning back to victim: "What am I supposed to do when my wife hates sex and makes a federal case out of even talking about it?"

Notice that these two kept shifting around in the roles of victim, rescuer, and persecutor. They are playing the basic game with the three roles any two people can take. **So long as they remain in one role, there can be no game. But if either changes roles, the game is on.** For example, if the man had stayed in the role of persecutor and she had stayed in the role of victim, he would have continued to blame her, and she would have continued to accept the blame. Such is what should have happened if he had been telling the truth and she really were to blame. There would have been a good chance to become partners in solving the problem: no more blame. However, since she was not to blame, and he was not telling the truth, he changed roles from persecutor to rescuer and, when she responded to that, the game was on. She then got angry and became the persecutor. He switched to victim. They will go on and on like this, since playing this game or any game resolves nothing. It simply inflicts more and more hurt and pain on the participants. The conflict has gotten out of control, as evidenced by the affair.Third-degree burns are being inflicted. Their marriage is going up in flames.

This basic game of victim-persecutor-rescuer also goes on in less dramatic ways. For example: a person snaps at his wife for being on the phone too long. (persecutor) She snaps back that he is domineering and arrogant. (persecutor) He goes into a righteous pout. (victim) The game is on. Later she apologizes (rescuer), but he says, "It's about time you admitted you were wrong." (persecutor)

Phony baloney can break out over saltshakers and toothpaste, just as easily as it can happen over sex, money, children, religion, in-laws, friends, use of time, choice of activities, where to live, or hat job to take. When couples continue to play games that hurt their feelings (all games burn), hurt and anger build up, killing off their feelings of love little by little. When they play more serious games, heir feelings of love die more quickly. The most serious games are those of affairs and divorce

Affairs and Divorce: The Deadliest Games

Affairs always involve the basic game. The one having the affair is the persecutor. Their partner s the victim. Another way of looking at it would be to portray or image the affair as killing the arriage by killing the feelings that led to marriage and that sustain the motivation for marriage. Either way affairs constitute third-degree burns. Those who have had affairs offer various reason for having them.

- To get even
- To find out if another person is more interesting or more loving than their spouse.
- To serve a "wake-up call" to their partner.
- To spice up their sex life.
- To force a crisis in the marriage.
- To make their partner jealous.
- To provoke their partner into filing for divorce.

Have you felt or do you feel any of these sentiments? If so, they are the first warning signs that our marriage is in serious trouble. An affair could be imminent. If any of these warning signs are present and the right person happens into your life, the stage is set for an affair.

Divorce can be as hurtful as an affair or even more hurtful, as victims of divorce can so eloquently confirm. While there are exceptions, most divorces are hurtful or even hateful rejections by at least one of the spouses. It is a devastating attack when one spouse rejects the other, perhaps the worst of all when the divorce blindsides the other partner.

If you are in a new marriage after having been divorced, learn from what happened. If you or partner had an affair, learn from it. If you have faced neither of these dreadful situations, count your blessings and learn from those who have experienced these situations.

The couple in our example could have avoided making the affair even more destructive to hem and their marriage if they had gone about it differently. Like this: he calls her one morning to tell her he has wronged her and is sorry. Since she would probably find out from looking at the mail before he got home, he just wanted her to know he was worried and would talk about it with her in the evening. When he gets home that evening, he tells her what he did and the reasons, which included unhappiness, dissatisfaction, and resentment over her approach to their sex life. He adds that since he has been too cowardly to get this conflict out in the open, he has no right to claim that his affair washer fault.

"I want to blame you, honey. But I really must blame myself." He admits that he was wrong not to be honest about the problem. He also admits that he has no right to an affair for any reason. He asks for her forgiveness and promises to end the affair and to seek professional therapy and counseling.

She is shocked and devastated. "Give me a little time to think and pray. I'm going to need counseling too. I want to hate you, and I am very hurt. Let's get help."

Takeaway

Sometimes you may be surprised that what you think is happening in your marriage may not be happening. Feedback from each other as spouses can never be too much. It is invaluable.

A good way to receive and give feedback about games is to do it nonverbally. Start with one hundred pennies. Whenever either of you thinks the other one is starting a game or inflicting hurt, put a penny into your jar. When the pennies are all gone, consider the results. The one whose jar has the most pennies has experienced the most episodes of hurt. The one with the fewest pennies has experienced the least number of hurtful episodes. If you wish to be more specific, agree to take a penny when experiencing hurt from the other one at the exact time the hurt was detected! That saves arguing about when the hurt occurred and what exactly was the hurtful deed. You might discover, for example, that there are words or deeds being received as a hurt when the one doing them does not even realize that something they say or do is hurting their partner.

NINE
BOUNDARY WORK: MEETING NEEDS FOR CLOSENESS AND DISTANCE

You may be surprised that there could be too much closeness in marriage and too little distance. It is no surprise that boundary problems are common in marriage. We each have our own personal space. Closeness is a way of sharing that space with others, whether physically, emotionally, or intellectually. You can hug me (physical), listen to my feelings (emotional), or discuss what we have read (intellectual). **Connecting is closeness. Not connecting is distance.** There are degrees of intensity in closeness and degrees of separateness in distancing. Hugging is closer than being listened to. Not making eye contact and not acknowledging a single word you say to me is more distant than simply nodding instead of replying to what the other person says.

Long before married people met each other their needs for closeness were already well established.

Closeness needs can be thought of as "oneness" needs, the opposite of feeling lonely or separate from others. These needs and tolerances vary a great deal from person to person. The need for oneness can be nearly total in you but nearly nonexistent within your spouse at any given time. How often do we hear the other person say, "Just leave me alone" or "Please hold and hug me?" Not only do these needs occur randomly, they also vary in intensity and duration, from person to person, and within each person. When experiencing stress, a person's need for closeness may intensify, while, when relaxed, that same person might cherish being left completely alone. A person who has an early total need for closeness will rarely like being alone. Being alone would mostly be boring. By way of contrast, the person who most of the time wants separateness would prefer being alone and working alone. Over the long run, most people strike a balance between these two needs. When a couple do not strike a balance that works for both of them, they will experience either enmeshment or alienation.

Enmeshment: Too Much Closeness

Closeness begins with life itself. From the time our mother conceived us, we were in asymbiotic relationship with her. After birth, that relationship continued emotionally: we bonded to our mother and were emotionally close, demanding as much of her time and attention as she could possibly give. It is not until sometime around the age of two that a second need begins to be operative: the need to **not** be close with our mother. From that point on, closeness and separateness are both enjoyable, very strong needs that can never be satisfied at the same time. Watch the child closely: the child will want to be held, but quickly want to be put down put then very quickly want to be picked up and held: two needs, diametrically opposite. **The longer one need is satisfied, the stronger becomes the opposite need.**

It is around these two needs that our relationship patterns get organized, with the closeness needs being met through shared space, acts of kindness, loving attention, nurture, and all things "loving."

Our culture defines love as "being with" and wanting to be with when apart from our "loved ones." When an adult with very high needs for "being with" gets married, "high needs for closeness" may actually turn into enmeshment. When this happens, it is often sexual in nature. The physical togetherness is nearly nonstop. The couple is so close that much of the time they look like one body with two heads. Driving down the highway all that is visible are two heads on the driver's side of the front seat.

Eventually, it will become obvious that one of them has a stronger need for closeness: that one takes control. The other one will begin feeling attacked, captured, taken over, devoured, trapped. A battle erupts or smolders over how much sex, how much physical closeness, how much "love" is too much. The couple are challenged to begin their sexual adjustment and all other forms of togetherness as well. But with enmeshment, it becomes impossible to "adjust" because, for at least one of the partners, the need for closeness is constant. This is the couple who always go together when they shop, when they attend social events, when they go to church, play tennis, go swimming, go visiting, go anywhere and do anything.

Power and control are concentrated in the hands of the partner needing the relationship to be literally a merger. That partner has taken over the marriage at the other partner's expense. Beware when you start to hear messages like these over and over:

- "When you are not here, I get depressed."
- "If you are upset, I am upset."
- "You make me happy."
- "I just want what is good for you."
- "Tell me what you are thinking."
- "Where have you been? I've been worried about you."
- "Who were you with?"
- "Who did you go to lunch with?"
- "What did the boss want?"
- "Who just called?"

- "Who have you been calling?"

It's Not jealousy

You may be tempted to think that it is only jealousy prompting the enmeshment patterns of behavior. That is because the comments will be expressed as jealousy. Jealousy is flattering and assuring. It reminds you that your partner still loves you, or that you still feel very strongly for your partner when you are the object of the jealousy. You may also be tempted to conclude that it is merely a matter of possessiveness, the desire to control, a power struggle. The comments and behaviors will be expressed as possessive, controlling, or manipulative. But the pattern is more than that.

"I wish you would call me when you know I'm so worried."

"You know I don't like for you to take chances."

"Don't make a move until you check with me. Otherwise, I'll be too upset. Don't surprise me. Don't shock me. Don't scare me. Take care of yourself, you are all that I have."

Sometimes the comments and behaviors will seem to be loving and caring when, in fact, they are invasions of privacy:

- Your partner plans a day off for you, without asking, because he or she "knows" that you are tired. (Enmeshed)

- You make a doctor's appointment for your partner because you are sure that he or she needs a checkup. You are being invasive.
- Your partner tells the boss to ease up on you. (Insulting)
- You open and read each other's personal mail and messages without asking. (Both of you are being too close and invasive.)
- You answer each other's phone messages without asking. (Both are being too close.)

Sometimes Retirement Triggers the Problem.

Often enough, enmeshment occurs when one partner has been out of the workforce for years before the other partner retires. Upon retirement, the person who retires decides to make up for lost time with the partner who has been home alone all this time. He or she all but shadows the partner who has been "home alone" by "going crazy" with love and affection all over again like when they were first married. Sometimes the "reinvigorated" newly retired partner becomes "overly helpful" by rearranging the cupboards, the drawers, the furniture, their social life, and their budget. They are "rescuing" their partner, even to the point of taking over with their partner's friends instead of finding new friends for themselves.

Each form of enmeshment, be it jealousy, control,

possessiveness, super caring, or taking too many liberties, needs to be seen for what it is: invasion. Left unchecked, it easily leads to big problems, including worries that one or the other wants out of the relationship.

When You Are the "Enmesher"

When you are the one invading your spouse or partner's territory in any of the way just described, you must practice self-discipline, learning to hold your tongue. Let go of your partner. Remind yourself that you do not own your partner. Further, you are not responsible for your partner's feelings or level of inner happiness, turmoil, or depression. You are your partner's partner, not your partner's mother or father.

If you find yourself worrying too much about your mate, **stop worrying.** Go to bed, go to sleep, dream about happy activities, get interested in new avenues for creativity, and constructive activity. **Detach** from thinking that you cannot survive without spending all your time with your partner. If you cannot readily do these things, seek professional assistance until you are able to be your own person. Allow your partner to be an individual with a life of their own, not just a shared life without. If all your spoken words about you and your partner are "we," you may be enmeshed. How about some "I" and "me" words? You are not being selfish to speak and think about yourself. It is not wrong to take care of yourself.

Alienation

Alienation in marriage is privacy that has run out of control. Privacy is pulling back inside of one's self in order to round up our thoughts, have our own space, be an individual.

But alienation is much more: a cold war breaks out in which one views their partner as personal threat. If this is you, you wish to escape from your partner almost all of the time. You try to keep your partner from knowing what you are thinking, what you are doing, where you have been, where you are going, what you are planning, how you are feeling, what you are experiencing. Your to achieve almost total control over the interaction between you and your partner in order to limit your relationship both in scope and in frequency of interaction and connecting.

For example: "Don't ask me any more questions about our taxes, ever again. Or "What you don't know won't hurt you." Or "I don't have time to talk with you at work. Don't call me."

Alienation also carries a high component of resentment, very little of which is revealed. You may resent your spouse for wanting more children or not wanting more children, spending too much money, not enjoying sex more, canceling the ski trip or hot tub, or wanting to join a new church. The possibilities for resentment are practically limitless. By nurturing, harboring, hiding, or holding in your resentment, you put even more distance between you and your mate.

The reasons for your resentment do not cause alienation. What causes alienation is **your failure to finish** the resentment. Either give in openly to your spouse or have the quarrel, clear the air and put it to rest once and for all as a **finished** conflict.

The more alienation that you build up towards your spouse, the more you make him or her the number one enemy in life. As you do this, your marriage relationship begins to change from love to hate. Just because you keep saying the words, "I love you" and keep calling your spouse by endearing words does not mean you are not alienated. Words of endearment and speeches of love cannot hide alienation. They certainly cannot stop it. The **work** of love, not the words of love, are what it takes.

Some symptoms of alienation include you spending increasing amounts of time away from your loved one. If you prefer to spend all of Saturday and Sunday away from your spouse when you have a choice, you may be alienated. When you enjoy and prefer being with your friends more than your partner, you are alienated. When you can hardly wait to enjoy leisure time with your friends, excluding your partner, you are alienated. When your spouse serves as a damper on your fun and a downer on the activities that you enjoy with your friends, you are alienated. When you or your spouse are constantly a drag, spoilsport, wet blanket, or naysayer, you are alienated.

When you start to feel ashamed, embarrassed, harassed, burdened, obligated, trapped, hemmed in, held down, and in general worse off for having your spouses as a spouse, you are alienated.

Alienation destroys a relationship just as much as does enmeshment. It is eventually a death knell to the marriage or commitment if not corrected. It sets in motion "falling out of love." It leads people to remark, "I don't know what it was that ever made me love him/her in the first place." It leads to one spouse being a deadweight while the other spouse is alive and thinking. Sometime sit leads to both spouses being deadweights.

There is a Cure

The cure for alienation is to do what should have been done to prevent alienation in the first place: putting resentment, anger, fears, conflict, unfinished quarrels out on the table and clearing the air—usually with your minister or a professional marriage therapist. You do not, at this point, do it all at once either, any more than you would melt an iceberg all at once. Then a courtship must be developed: learn to enjoy some activities together, resume communicating about personal topics and, most importantly, get back to work on the **7th contract**, category by category, for as long as it takes.

In order to recommit, you must rekindle your love. In order to rekindle your love, you must reorganize your marriage relationship so that it is rewarding and fulfilling instead of burdensome. Once again, get back to work on that **7th contract.** It takes considerable time to correct alienation in marriage, months if not years. The cure is both relational and personal. As a rule of thumb, the longer either or both of you have been closed down to the other, the more advisable it would be to involve a professional third party for help to change the situation. Anger is almost always involved in marital distancing that has gotten out of control. Some of the anger will be at self, too, since extreme separateness stirs us up to rage at ourselves as we did when we were children.

The "doctor's advice" for this problem is not all bad: pay more attention to boundary work. Respect one another's boundaries. Realize that you are each individuals who need separateness as well as closeness. Do not wait to resume your sex life if that has stopped. Use sex as part of the healing process: something sex is intended to do. Figure out good ways to communicate your needs for both closeness and separateness. Be fine-tuned to your partner's signals, and make sure that you give your signals loud and clear.

TEN
NUTURE, NUTURE, NUTURE

———————❧———————

Is yours a nurturing marriage or a troubled marriage?

D o you feel good living in your family right now? Do you feel you are living with loved ones who love you? Is it fun and exciting to be a member of your family, and do you have friends in your family? If you answered "yes" to all three questions, you live in a nurturing family. If you answered "no" to any of them, you may live in a troubled family. Here are six ways to tell the difference between a nurturing and a troubled family, relationship, or marriage;

1. The atmosphere

One indication of a **troubled** marriage is that the atmosphere is too polite. No one ever offends anybody, but life with each other is so boring because there is no feeling. You may be perfectly correct with one another, answering each question asked, speaking when spoken to, answering each question asked, but that's all. Such politeness is a mask of veiled hostility and resentment. One shuts down one's emotions by becoming overly polite.

In a **nurturing relationship,** love and support are communicated all the time. You feel good being around each other. Your children and friends feel good being with you. Like a warm winter fire, it's nice to be there. The formal, phony, over-politeness is not present. Family members aren't jumpy about convention and are not easily offended. They can be themselves.

2. Secrecy

In a **troubled** family, secrecy abounds. The first words a professional hears are often," Please do not tell my partner that I have been here to get help. I don't want him or or her to know." The family climate has too much secrecy. Keeping secrets is a stressor, in addition to being a sign of very low trust levels.

In a **nurturing** climate, anything can be talked about with anyone. There is plenty of listening and being listened to. I remember one family coming to see me. The teenage son had been called into the principal's office for some outlandish behavior. Since he had been a model student, what he had done was totally out of character. Fearing some great change of personality, the principal immediately recommended professional counseling. The boy refused to come for counseling unless both parents came with him. In they came. Once the three of them were seated, the boy looked at me, laughed, and announced: "I have done my job, Doc, now you do yours!" With that, he left. He was simply trying to get Mother and Dad to open up to each other. Since all else had failed, he got himself into trouble at school in order to get his parent into counseling. Smart boy!

If you find that there is a secretive climate in your marriage and family, start today sharing those secrets, making sure to not violate trust or anyone's ethical responsibilities. Begin by telling one secret every day until there is no more secrecy. Listen and be listened to by your partner and children, if there are children. No more anyone saying "No, nothing is bothering me" when being asked what is wrong. You and all others, including your partner, will feel better doing this. Do not believe the advice that it is better not to worry anyone else with your worries. Those you live with need to know even when they can't help. For them not to know is for them to imagine the worst or to conclude that they are not significant enough for you to bother with, i.e., you really do not care about them.

3. Troubled marriages make for **stressful** homes: the bodies of those living in stress are physically stiff and tight or slouchy. People's faces look sullen, dull, dank, sad, anything but alive and thrilled.

In a nurturing climate, the bodies and faces tell the whole story: they are graceful, relaxed, moving, alert. Even the house has lots of light and color. It's a place where people live. It is planned for comfort and joy. It is okay to have friends over. It's okay to be noisy and rattle around the pots and pans, to kick off the shoes and put the feet up, to toss a few logs into the fireplace, pull a few more chairs onto the veranda, to relax. Most times somebody is doing just that! If your home has fallen victim to over-cleanliness, become a museum of sorts, if it is tooneat and too well-kept for others to feel comfortable, lower your standards. Start with aa room in which you think you would be the most comfortable. Fill up one area afteranother with laughter and nurture, until your whole house is a joy to be in.

Two rooms in most homes are the most important because we spend so much time in them: the kitchen and the bedroom. Rest and love come into the bedroom. Food and love come into the kitchen. **These are the two places where there should never be an argument.** When you disagree, get out of these two rooms and stay out until the argument is resolved. What happens in these two rooms impacts our moods every day. Test both of these rooms for yourself: if you do not feel better just being in them, not enough good things are happening there. That means it is time to get some good things going on in these two nurturing places.

For example:

- Make doing the dishes a nurturing experience. Get the kids involved if you have children. Make sure to clown and have fun a little while you are at it. Make sure that both you and your partner do the dishes together.
- Get some music going?
- Bring in some fresh flowers.
- Be sure to kiss each other every time you go into either of these rooms.

4. In troubled relationships, voices are either **harsh or barely audible.** When people speak, it is often intended to hurt, condemn, criticize, and show anger. The rest of the time, people are trying to be subdued or not be noticed.

In nurturing marriages, there is a great amount of happy noise. Voices go up and down all the time. People shout, laugh, scream, chuckle, and make all sorts of meaningful noises. Quiet comes too, but it is natural, peaceful, truly quiet.

Listen closely in your home: does it sound like a library, hospital, or funeral home instead of happy place where happy people live? If it is too quiet, start making some noise and stop signaling others in your home to be quiet.

5. In a troubled **relationship**, there is little evidence of **friendship or joy**. Staying together is mostly out of duty. If you are staying together for the sake of the children until the children are grown, you are tolerating each other.

In a **nurturing** relationship, persons are comfortable touching one another and showing affection. They **like** being together. They have fun when together. Be it popcorn or snowballs, storms or sunshine, lawn parties or card games, Sunday evening walks, or early morning breakfasts, when there is nurturing there is fun. We feel liked, and we do a lot of liking. If this is not happening in your home, it's never too late to get started. When it does happen, notice how catchy friendship and joy can be. Give someone in your home a hug every day. Make your partner some coffee. Have breakfast in bed. Hold hands while watching TV.

6. In a troubled marriage, there is little **humor**. What humor there is tends toward bitter, sarcastic, cruel, and cutting. Put-downs and pessimistic "gallows laugh" type of comments pass for jokes.

In a **nurturing** marriage, funny things are truly funny. There is lots of laughter and no hurt. You won't need to look up jokes in a book to find laughing matters.

Self-Worth Impacts Our Ability to Nurture

When we feel like we matter, the world appears to be a better place. When we appreciate our own worth, it is easy to notice and respect the worth of others. Integrity, honesty, responsibility, compassion, love, support, and communication come naturally. We find it easy to accept our feelings and share them. We recognize crisis points as only temporary. We are more confident of our problem-solving ability. We have confidence that, with our loved ones, combining our strengths and good points, we will survive most any adversity.

In a troubled climate, this is not the case. We feel little personal worth, expecting to be cheated, stepped on, taken advantage of, overlooked, ignored, not taken seriously. We expect the worst. Distrust will breed loneliness and isolation, which in turn will bring on depression and discouragement. Then come apathy and indifference. We stop caring about self and others. We ignore our health needs, nutrition, exercise, eventually even our grooming, and just about all of our fun.

Be assured, if your nurturing quotient is low, so is that of your partner and any others who make up your family. It simply does not happen otherwise: if one of you is non-nurturing so are the rest of you. If one of you is communicating love and support, so is the partner and any others in your family. Believe that you can improve your relationships and then get started doing what works: the work of love.

Foster Integrity and Compassion

The way to foster integrity and compassion is to be open with your partner, children, loved ones, and friends. Believe what your partner tells you—many times a day—in simple little ways:

"I'm tired." Respond with a pillow, not a pep talk about aerobic exercise.

"I'm discouraged." Respond with a question about why that is, not a positive mental attitude slogan.

"I'm afraid." Respond by holding or hugging your partner, not by declaring there is no reason to feel that way.

"I'm getting a bad feeling about the boss." Respond by listening, not by defending the boss or criticizing your partner.

"I feel so alone and like a failure when I get sick and when I am disagreed with." Responding with compassion, "I will always be with you" is so different than "Don't be a baby, don't be so silly." Give lots of hugs, especially when your partner is telling you that he or she needs hugging right away.

Compassion, by the way, derives from the Latin word meaning to care intensely about what the other person is experiencing. Compassion is a sharing in another person's experience. Hugging is not analyzing but **feeling** with the other person. When we nurture, we are being compassionate. That means listening, holding, comforting, caring, doing for. That means asking how the other person is feeling and then listening for the answer.

Foster Honesty and Trust

Tell the truth: if you mean you are angry, do not say that you have a headache. If you mean that you are tired of being together with your spouse today, say so. If you really missed your mate while he or she was away on a business trip, say so instead of acting hurt and playing victim.

Foster Responsibility by Being Responsible

As a couple and as a family, divide up such things as doing dishes, laundry, and vacuuming. Then also banking, paying bills, emptying the trash, servicing the vehicles, bringing in the paper and the mail. Do these things on time, cheerfully, thoroughly, every time.

As a couple, it is your responsibility to protect and defend each other's good name. Be sure to admire, respect, trust, and be pleasing for each other. If there are reasons why you cannot do these things, address those reasons honestly and openly. Never make jokes about each other to anyone else. Do not run each other down to others, ever. Do not air dirty linen out to the public and not to your children. Keep your loyalties in perspective. The words "above all others" always apply.

Are Mistakes Legal in Your Marriage?

Are mistakes legal in your relationship? They are "legal" if, in response to each other's mistakes, there is patience and support to take care of the damage, which can be anything from spilling milk to costly financial mistakes. Mistakes are illegal in your relationship if they are met with judgment, criticism, and blame. In a nurturing relationship, one does not "catch hell" for forgetting a birthday, scratching the car, crumpling a fender, backing into the garage door, or getting a traffic ticket.

Blame and criticism messages can come in subtle ways such as eyebrows raised, looks on the face, tone of voice. They can also be obvious: "Can't you do anything right? Why don't you do what ask? Put some effort into it!" Pay attention. When you feel yourself anxious, nervous, worried, afraid of what your partner's reaction will be, it signals that mistakes are indeed illegal, a big weakness in your relationship.

What effect does this have on your marriage? The more your mistakes are objected to or condemned by the one who is supposed to love you most, the more you will feel that **you,** not just the mistake, are being condemned. Making mistakes illegal creates the danger that your being loved becomes conditional on your attempts to be goof-proof. Conditional love is, of course, not love at all. It is rejection and hostility disguised as love. It is a subtle message that you are not acceptable, esteemed, or desirable the way you are. It is a demand that you be some other way if you wish to be loved. It means that the **7th contract** needs to be revisited! Start new habits:

- With speaking mistakes, say "I love you" when your spouse calls one of the children by the wrong name or garbles a sentence or says the wrong thing about your weight.
- With action mistakes, say "I love you" when your spouse scrapes a fender, leaves tire tracks on the new lawn, or drops a prized dish.
- With mental mistakes, say "I love you" when your spouse forgets an anniversary, reads the map wrong, gets lost, or makes a mess out of the income tax returns.
- With spiritual mistakes, say "I forgive you."

Appreciate your Differences

I point out to couples that in a "successful" marriage, both people constantly work in support of the life goals of each, not just the shared goals of both as enunciated in the categories of money, sex, children, use of time, choice of activities, dealings with extended family, and spirituality. The net effect is that they, in many ways, become more and more different because each person is unique. As they look back, they will notice that they have not only grown together around the items in the 7th contract, but they each have also become more and more of who they were meant to be as unique persons. Ideally, they would be able to say that being married has helped each of them become more of who they are, as compared to doing life alone because there were always both of them supporting each other in their life goals. In some ways, they became more alike. In other ways, they became more different.

Big trouble comes when a couple cannot accept differences in each other. I am not talking about criminal activity, gross habits, offensive behaviors, or character flaws. These should be mutually acknowledged and worked at together for improvement. But with legitimate differences, the challenge is to accept and learn to appreciate differences, resisting the temptation to try changing one's partner. The list of those things can be long and tempting. It can include eating habits, work habits, choice of jobs, financial thinking, approach to sex, religious beliefs, parenting style, ways of dressing, choice of friends, and health habits.

The test of true nurture is not just mistakes that are forgiven but also differences that are accepted.

ELEVEN
SEASONS OF A MARRIAGE: WHAT
TO EXPECT

Marriage could be thought of as having four seasons that more or less correspond to four eras of adulthood: The **Founding Years ages 18–35**

The Launch Years   **ages 35–50**

The Empty Nest Years **ages 50–65**

The OLDER YEARS   **ages 65+**

The First Season of Marriage: Age 18 to 35. The Founding Years

By about age 35, boys and girls become men and women. In the process, they face the challenge of validation. Validation includes becoming convinced that we are attractive, pleasant to be with, competent, and capable. It also includes coming to believe that we are admirable, lovable, worthwhile, self-directing, and trustworthy. There is no guarantee that any of us will come to such conclusions about ourselves, only that those who do so will need statistically about 35 years to do it and, with men, a few more years than women.

"Validation" originates from the praise and feedback of our parents, teachers, and peers. Test results and evaluations, job performance reviews, awards, citations, and comments from friends all contribute toward validation. Validation by others could be thought of as votes. Unlike voting, however, the positive feedback in our favor is relatively meaningless unless and until we accept it. With women who have not been validated by their father, it is very difficult to accept validation. With men who have failed at school or sports, it is also very difficult to accept validation.

Using the analogy of voting, the vote that matters is the last vote to be cast: our own vote. Some people never cast that vote. Others need help to do so and take longer. But statistically speaking, by age35 most adults are at least beginning to believe in themselves. Until then, young couples continue with at least some of what went on in dating: each putting the best foot forward and not all that confident about how long their partner will love them. Being loved by another person is, in fact, a super validation, but for the loved one who does not believe in their own worth, it only goes to show how wonderful is the lover!

One must live quite some time before internalizing the reality that I am lovable, and that is why my partner loves me. A woman knows she is validated and has cast her own vote when she can honestly say that anyone who does not love her needs their head examined. Until then, if her partner hesitates about loving her, she will wonder what is it about herself that is not lovable. The same holds true for the man.

When a married couple are experiencing validation issues, they are also living through the first season of their marriage: **falling in love, founding their marriage, and filling the nest.** They work to establish a secure home or rental, solidify their career or job, start a family if they wish to have children, and learn how to be married. This is a time when they discover much of what lies in their unwritten contracts and hammer out what their "deal" is actually going to be: the 7th contract. If they have children, this is the time during which they fill up the nest. It is also the time during which they solidify their dealings with their extended families and friends, and develop affiliations with church if they wish to be church members.

The Second Season of Marriage: Ages 35 to 50. The Launch or Emptying the Nest

As you raise your children towards independence, you will increasingly think about launching them. The launch years also include grooming successors at work, getting new blood into the organizations and causes with which you are involved, and finding more ways to get away for peace and quiet. Your nest become too busy, too crowded, too demanding. You feel the burdens.

By this time, you will begin to notice that the two of you married quite young. What started out from the adolescent doubting point of view, "Would he or she still love me if . . ." gradually becomes "I can't worry about that now. It's not my problem." This happens for good reason. Taking care of your figure, your outward appearance, your spirit, and your responsibilities started out as a way to please your partner. But, as the validation process takes stronger hold, the reason becomes **that you deserve this for you.**

As you accept validation, your reason for being married becomes even more that you are married in order to **share** your goodness, love and happiness, rather than getting happiness and love from your mate. So long as either of you do not believe in yourself, there will be insecurity in your married relationship. During this second season of marriage, you will likely need to get this big issue settled.

Are you going to hang on to each other emotionally, or are each of you going to stand on your own two feet? Will you be strong, confident, sharing partners who believe in yourselves? Or are you going to be needy of each other, constantly controlling, dependent, unable, and unwilling to be a person? Will you believe in yourself and claim your own happiness and purpose?

About this time in life, if you believe in God, you will come to realize that God has always cast his vote for you, then came votes from your parents and spouse, then finally your vote.

Crisis Times

With children, the launch years in marriage become a series of sagas: getting them through secondary school, getting them through college, getting them properly licensed to drive a vehicle, getting them through puppy loves, helping them stay on the right side of the law, to name a few. There are also changes in the friends who once crowded your schedule and your married life. Some of those friends move or drift away or get sick and die. There are funerals and weddings, graduations, promotions, demotions, retirements. There may be the loss of your parents or close relatives, moves to a new neighborhood, becoming a grandparent, facing serious health challenges with yourself, your spouse, or both of you. When the dust settles, the third season of marriage begins.

The Third Season of Marriage: Age 50 to 65. The Empty Nest Years

The empty nest years refer to those years when the children are grown and gone, roughly starting at about age 50. The challenge of these years is to find new meaning and purpose in your marriage that has been organized until now around your family.

If you went to work each morning in order to earn money for supporting your children, that purpose is now gone. If you hurried home to cook for your children, that too is now gone. Weekends will no longer be filled with laughing children; evenings will be quiet. The house will be neat and, wonder of wonders, the refrigerator will have food in it! The kitchen will be neat. In fact, the whole house will be neat and orderly— and you may not like that one single bit!

It is a shock to experience the emptiness of a home whose children have grown and gone. Further, with the growing up of your children comes the loss of friends related to the children's activities. Some families at this point realize they no longer need both parents to continue working. Sometimes early retirement also becomes possible. But the question becomes: early retirement? For what?

This is the point in time when many women go back to school or begin second careers. One of the many new challenges you may face as a couple is that of Dad wanting to retire earlyand move away to a resort area, while Mom is just getting started in a promising new career.

Until this period of time in your marriage, everything

was future oriented. Some day children would be raised. Someday there would be less stress and strain. Someday you could get back to being married. Some day in the future has become "now." You may feel empty, bewildered, and somewhat puzzled as to what is now worthwhile. For those couple who do not have children the nest also feels empty as the children of your friends grow up and leave, and their parents move away or begin to die. The issues become the same as for couples who raised children: "Now what?"

Remember this as you search for the answer: **at age 50 you have been an adult for only30 years**. You may have 50 more years of adulthood ahead of you. Conceivably, your marriage is not even half over at this point. You are not old, and this is by no means the end. It is only the end of chapter, not the end of the book!

Any unfinished business regarding validation and identity needs continued work. Sometimes people who make it this far begin to think about divorce. In spite of constant advice to contrary, many other people stick it out in unsatisfactory marriages for the sake of the children. The empty nest may seem like the right time to bail out and start over on your own or with someone else.

The better way, if possible, would be to map a new future for yourselves as a couple. After all, it is **your** future. You both own your marriage. You can make of it whatever you wish. The future lies at your feet to do with as you wish, to give yourselves to new tasks and new purpose. The key is **new purpose**, something that otherwise is likely not on your map.

Do not be tempted to think that now you can retire and enjoy unending leisure. You will bore ourselves. Besides, there are too many people who need you. Now you are free to get into worthy causes, to volunteer, to study more about world problems such as hunger and injustice. Now you have become adults with a great deal of wisdom and experience. You are relatively free and maybe financially secure. Use your good fortune creatively and lovingly. That is the secret to a happy future, a future that is important enough for you to carefully plan.

The Fourth Season: Age 65 and Beyond. The Older Years

The years ahead are unknown as to how many. There could be as many as 35 more years or more. How long we live and, therefore, how long our marriage will endure, depends increasingly on how hard we work at staying healthy. Certainly, health problems, health needs, and health care decisions will take up a significant amount of your time and energy. With increasing limitations due to to age, there will be an increasing need to plan carefully and choose wisely how to use time and energy. This is also a time when many more items in your "unwritten contracts" will come to light. After all, you each will have had 65 years to live and learn about end-of-life years. Know that someday, if you both live long enough, the end-of-life older years will be yours to share. Some items and issues on which to keep a close eye are:

- Do not let yourself get "warehoused." Plan meaningfully for long-term support and supportive living. Do what you can to keep your support system active.

- Pay attention to your health care directive, wills and any other wishes you may have regarding your end-of-life health care, and funeral.

- Continue to be productive and creative.

- Celebrate past events and high points of your life with one and all! You probably paid for these high points with blood, sweat, and tears, so "get your money's worth" out of them by sharing. Make this a time when you can look back and laugh about things that are only funny now!

Did you know that there are softball leagues that have a minimum age to join, beginning at age 55, 60, 70, 80, or 90 years?

Summary About the Seasons of Marriage

The seasons of marriage parallel to some degree the

seasons of life itself. Given the nearly endless variations of each person's life span, the same will be true of each marriage: variations. But just as with life itself, the idea in marriage is to live it until we die and do not rush the ending! Pay attention not only to what comes to light in your unwritten contract but also in that of your spouse.

Keep that **7th contract** up-to-date!

Make Frank Sinatra's song your song but in a slightly different way: "**But best of all, we did it our way!**"

TWELVE
MAY YOUR MARRIAGE BE BLESSED

Traditionally it was assumed that the newly married couple intended to have children. Part of the well-wishing included joining the couple in their desire for children. The prayer was that they would be blessed with children and live to see their children's children to the third and fourth generation. That is my wish and prayer for you, the reader, if that is what you hope for in your marriage. For all who read these words, I pray and wish for you the desires of your heart, whatever that may be. I hope that the concepts and approaches that I have shared with you will be helpful.

For some, it may be a challenge to accept that much of our behaviors are actually driven by less than conscious influences within ourselves. "Hidden forces within ourselves" may sound scary. The good news, however, is that what is hidden will come open if we know what to watch for and how to do it. That is what the notion of unwritten contracts is about: getting those hidden influences out into the open so that we can take account of them rather than be driven by them. Our culture would have us believe than romance is what marriage is all about. Commercially we are led to believe that the secret to a happy marriage lies with flowers, chocolates, loving cards, and romantic dinners. Great! Do it! But then get down to the work of love. That work goes on day and night.

To Those Not Sure About Getting Married

The focus of this book is on married couples; how to keep making their marriage stronger, happier, more fulfilling. The focus needed to be somewhere. But anyone contemplating getting married can use this book to decide if marriage is for them. It helps to know about the work of love: much better than "trial marriages." Not everyone is cut out for marriage. Once again, honesty in dating is the best policy. I stand strongly by the assertion that it is always important for people who plan to marry to do so out of love. Of course, it is important to be in love! The big point, however, is that the couple know how to do the work of love. That is what takes them well past their honeymoon years and builds a durable foundation under their love relationship.

Think of it this way: if I want to always love you, I would want to know how to get that to happen, and I would definitely want to do what it takes. Then I would also need to take stock: am Willing to do what it takes? Marriage, if done seriously, is a commitment to our partner that is forever, blind to the future, and no escape hatches. People of faith have God's promise to be with them through any and all of the hard times. Note: not a promise that there will not be hard times, just a promise to walk with us through our valleys.

We also expect that our family and friends will be with us in the valleys, not just on the mountaintops. Those who do not believe in God will need their friends and family all the more. "Private" marriages are not a good idea. Trial marriages are not a good idea. Conditional love is not a good idea. Reducing sexual sharing to a recreational option is not a good idea: because it turns partners into commodities to be shopped for, tried out, then thrown away when deemed no longer desirable.

Thank you for reading this book and, thereby, listening to my thoughts. That is always a compliment. I wish you the very best! If you would like to be on the site I plan to offer for readers of this book, please send me your email address. Mine is cuatulsa@cox.net.

God bless you.

Larry Losoncy

ADDITIONAL READING

The Structure of Magic: Bandler and Grinder

The How To of Forgiveness: Dr. Joan W. Ellason

Games People Play: Eric Berne

I'm Ok, You're OK: Thomas A. Harris

An Orgasm of Tears: Jayne M. Wesler

All Our Children: The American Family Under Pressure: Kenneth Keniston

Letters from Women Who Love Too Much: Robin Norwood

Why Am I Afraid to Love? And

Why Am I Afraid to Tell You Who I Am?: John Powell

Marriage Contracts and Couple Therapy: Dr. Clifford J. Sager

Co-Dependence Misunderstood: Anne Wilson Schaef

The Couples Treasure Chest: Dr. Richard Nongard

Seasons of a Marriage: H. Norman Wright

Made in the USA
Monee, IL
20 May 2021